# Contemporary BRITISH QUILT ART

## Christine Nelson

Dryad Press Ltd, London

**Acknowledgement**

The author would like to express her thanks to all those people whose work appears in this book, and to Mr Terry Waddington for photography work in relation to its production.

© Christine Nelson 1989
First published in 1989

ISBN 0 8521 9751 9

Typeset by Servis Filmsetting Ltd.
Printed and bound in Great Britain by
Hartnolls Ltd., Cornwall
for the Publishers
Dryad Press Ltd.
8 Cavendish Square
London W1M 0AJ

A CIP record for this book is available from the British Library.

# Contents

4

# Introduction

**Fig 1** The soft texture of a quilted surface

This book was prompted by the question, why and how do people create quilts in the late 1980s, and it aims to introduce the reader to new approaches in quiltmaking and to inspire experiment.

Generally, many people have become associated with quiltmaking for nostalgic and practical reasons and most people begin the craft by studying and copying historical examples. Traditional methods of working and the historical development of patchwork and quilting are therefore explained, so that changes which are happening presently can be related to work produced in the past. By knowing something of the historical makers, their inspiration, and the processes they invented and built on, we can increase our awareness of contemporary work. The sewing and quilting skills which are described offer the reader an introduction to the art of quiltmaking through a description of basic techniques which are illustrated with step-by-step drawings.

Making up a quilt from our own ideas allows us to express our individuality, and design techniques and interpretation for some experimental quilts are dealt with. By emphasising the main considerations, and using illustrated examples, the quiltmaker is encouraged to create personal designs for quilts which break away from the traditional.

In the past ten years quiltmaking has developed in an art context and twelve quilt artists who share a commitment to promote the art of quiltmaking, whilst retaining their own individual and professional style of work, explain their differing approaches in detail. The reader is able to share the inspiration for the quilts they produce and their unique working methods, which often combine traditional techniques with new inventive methods and subject matter.

# The historical development of patchwork and quilting

We live in a throwaway consumer society. Our goods, including our clothing, are relatively cheap and plentiful. Looking at patchwork and quilting produced in the past enables us to realise the value to former generations of cloth as a precious commodity, spun, woven, dyed and printed by hand. Fabrics are known to have existed in Neolithic times (6000 BC), in Anatolia, but, because of its perishable nature, comparatively little cloth remains from early days. The earliest known example of patchwork was found in the Cave of the Thousand Buddhas in India and dates from the sixth and seventh centuries AD. These earliest examples are known as applied work, where patches of fabric or leather are applied to a cloth background and held in place by stitchery.

The Crusaders of the eleventh and twelfth centuries are believed to have brought the art of patchwork to England from the Middle East, and quilted clothing was also used at this time as protection under armour. One of the oldest pieces of authentic English appliqué in England is at Stoneyhurst College, near Preston in Lancashire. It represents a knight clad in full armour mounted on a spirited galloping horse (Fig 2). The knight represents a Crusader since the cross, the insignia of the cause, is a prominent figure in the ornamentation of the knight's helmet, his shield, and on the blanket of his horse. The embroidery is thought to have been made in the thirteenth century. Also preserved from this period is the tattered fragment of a coat worn by Edward the Black Prince, a replica of which now hangs over his tomb in Canterbury Cathedral. The coat is of red and blue velvet applied to a calico background and closely quilted.

The original function of quilting was to provide warmth economically. In the British climate the sandwiching together of a warm layer of wool between two cloth covers fulfilled this need adequately. The Great Freeze of the fourteenth century altered ways of dressing and, after a desperately cold winter, extra bedcoverings were needed to provide warmth and comfort. At first, scraps saved from old clothes and furnishings were used to piece coverlets together, but when new materials began to be imported from the East during the seventeenth and eighteenth centuries, their variety changed the whole concept of patchwork into one of creative design.

After about 1650 Indian cottons were in great demand in England. The cloth was printed with fine designs, and good dyes were used on calico, which became a much used fabric. Calico was imported from Calicut on the South West coast of India. Chintz, derived from the Hindu word *chint*, meaning variegate, was also a popular cloth for furnishings. An English printing industry developed, using the traditional Indian imported designs, and by the middle of the eighteenth century thousands of bolts of cloth were being woven in Lancashire and sent down from Manchester for bleaching in the fields near London before printing.

The oldest known surviving example of English patchwork is the Levens Hall Coverlet at Kendal, made in 1708 from Indian calicos (Fig 3). During this time patchwork was a home craft undertaken by all classes of people. Girls were taught patchwork at a young age, together with sampling and needlework. This 'education' in sewing was linked to their future adult roles as housewives and mothers. The craft thrived, and some beautiful coverlets were made and became prized as heirlooms. However, not everyone saw value in the work. George Eliot expressed a dismal view of the craft in *The Mill on the Floss*. '"It's foolish work", said Maggie, with a toss of her mane. "Tearing things to pieces to sew 'em together again".'

English patchwork quilts have traditionally been made either from the centre of the quilt outwards with a large central panel framed by borders (Fig 4), or from one geometric pattern which made up the entire quilt, as used in the design called 'Grandmother's Flower Garden' (Fig 5). These hexagon patterns were, and continue to be, popular. The patches are

**Fig 2** Appliqué figure of a knight on horseback. English, thirteenth century

7

8

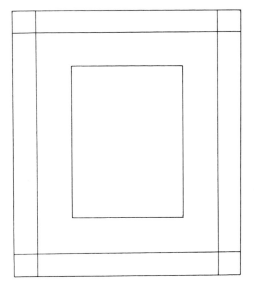

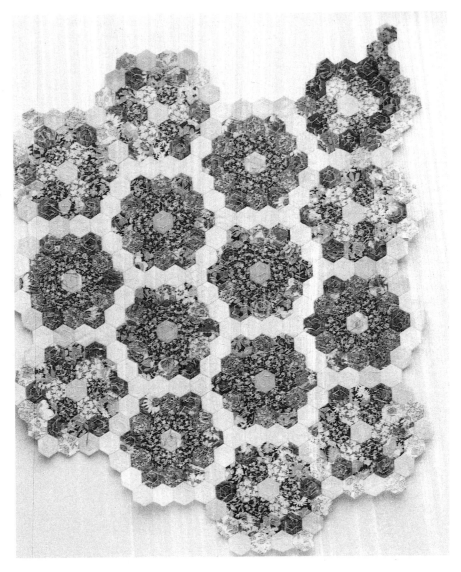

handsewn, and the method of making and joining them has come to be known as the English Method. Many of today's quiltmakers were introduced to patchwork hrough this way of working. Strip quilting is another traditional patchwork method which originated in England and Ireland. This consists of strips of fabric, which run the whole length of the quilt, sewn together. They may be of the same or of different widths, and sometimes they are padded and quilted individually.

Patchwork and quilting have recently come full circle, with the revival of interest and developments in American art quilts and quilt collecting influencing quilt design in Britain. It was the early American settlers from Britain and the Low Countries who imported the craft of quiltmaking. Cotton fabrics in America were imported, because the American cotton crop was not established until the 1720s, and weaving in the colonies was forbidden by the British. As a result, fabrics were expensive and carefully used. The way of life for settlers was hard, resulting in a group closeness and combined effort. Patchwork and quilting became a social and co-operative activity which still thrives at all levels.

Two major developments of American patchwork have influenced present-day quilters in Britain. First, the method of joining patches led naturally to adaptation once sewing machines were invented. Secondly,

**Fig 3** The first known surviving example of English patchwork: The Levens Hall Coverlet, 1708

**Fig 4** Traditional English patchwork quilt design

**Fig 5** Traditional English patchwork 'Grandmother's Flower Garden' design

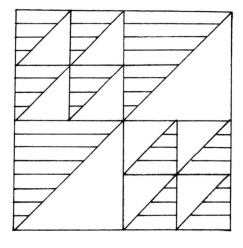

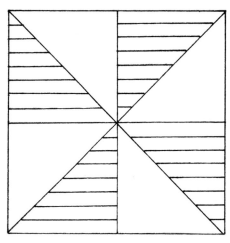

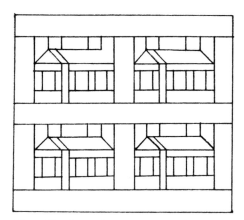

**Fig 6** Traditional American patchwork quilt designs: 'Flock of Geese', 'Windmill', 'Schoolhouse'

American quiltmakers contributed a new approach to quilt design by using quilt blocks. This involves organising small geometric units, such as squares, triangles and rectangles, into blocks which are then joined together to make a quilt (Fig 6). Some of these blocks are inspired by natural forms and are given names such as 'Bearspaw', 'Flock of Geese', etc, whilst some are inspired by everyday life, such as 'Windmill' and 'Schoolhouse'.

In Victorian times there was a fashion for making crazy quilts, which used irregular patches and fabrics of varying texture and colour. The finished work was elaborately decorated with stitchery and beadwork, and it was often used for door-curtains, cushions and sofa throws. By the First World War, with changes in women's work and status, the arts of quilting and patchwork nearly died out. However, they remained strong in some areas of the country, such as the North East and Wales, where women's society was sharply segregated from men's by the manual nature of men's work – shipbuilding and mining. There was a revival of interest in the craft in these areas during the Great Depression of the 1930s and a later revival by the Women's Institutes in Britain. About ten years ago a desire, felt by some sections of the population in Britain, to return to old values, coupled with concerns about the advance of technology, led to a nostalgic search for life based upon a simpler past. Victorian and earlier textile designs became popular, and there was a revival of quiltmaking which was influenced by these fashionable decorative design changes. The majority of people making quilts in Britain and America today are using the craft as a way of exploring personal artistic ideas and needs, in a time of rapid change.

Many modern quiltmakers have an interest and grounding in traditional patchwork and quilting. Great Britain has several rich and varied museum collections of patchwork and quilting, displaying a variety of techniques dating back to the eighteenth century. The quilts are often laboriously handpieced, but they show a surprising inventiveness, and there is also at times an artistry in colour and design which provides inspiration for new ideas.

A large collection of quilts at the Strangers Hall Museum, in Norwich, includes work dating from the eighteenth century, and many handsewn hexagon patchworks from the nineteenth century. In these quilts a wide variety of border patterns are employed, and the fineness of materials and sewing are an inspiration. Another important English collection is stored at the Victoria and Albert Museum in London, where quilts and coverlets of the eighteenth century are well represented, and there is an especially important group of about fifty patchwork quilts dating from the late eighteenth to the late nineteenth century. The works are a representative selection of the variety of textile patterns produced in different periods. There are some beautiful silk quilts, including one dating from the eighteenth century made up of silk ribbons pieced in a simple block pattern. A study of these collections reveals to us how historic patchwork is quintessentially related to its makers.

The American Museum in Britain at Claverton, near Bath, has an interesting collection of patchwork, appliqué and quilting which relates to American history and tradition. It includes Amish quilts and varied examples of patchwork which have beautiful controlled pattern and colour effects within the print areas. The nature of the display confirms that the size and scale of the bed quilts is important by making it possible to 'read' the pattern effectively.

# Basic techniques of patchwork and quilting

To the beginner, making a large quilt can seem a formidable project, but, given a basic knowledge of patchwork and quilting techniques, it is possible to sample out small ideas and discover which methods have personal appeal.

### The traditional English method of joining patches

This is the method used for handsewing, not only hexagonal patches, but also triangles, squares, rectangles, and octagons. A paper template is required for each patch to be joined, and is made by drawing round a card, metal or plastic template. Metal and plastic templates are long-lasting and accurate, which is important. Cut out the drawn paper templates and pin them to a piece of cotton or firmly-woven fabric with one edge along the straight grain (Fig 7a). Cut the fabric with a 1 cm seam allowance, turn the seam allowance in, and tack the paper to the fabric (Fig 7b). Press the individual patches to give a crisp edge. Join the patches by turning them right sides together and sewing along the edges to be joined with small regular oversewing stitches (Fig 7c). The colour of thread used is traditionally white, and the stitches show slightly on the right side, which gives the patchwork a characteristic appearance.

**Fig 7** The traditional English method of joining patches

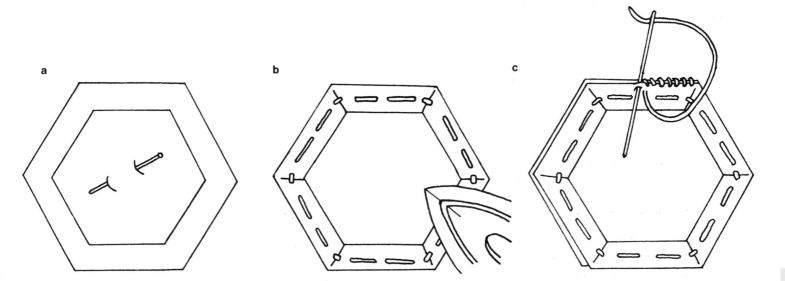

a         b         c

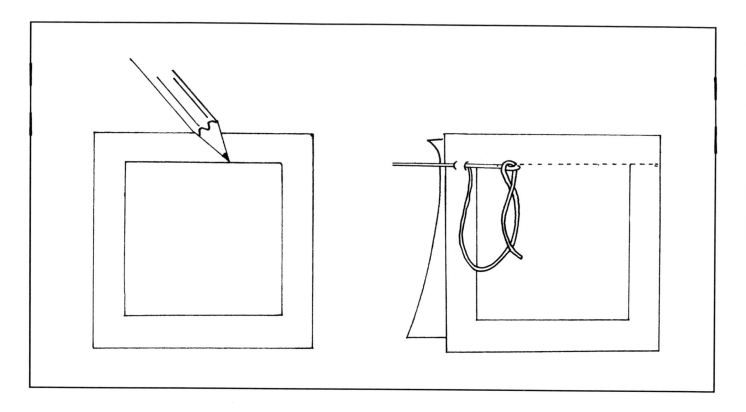

## The American method of joining patches

The traditional American method of sewing patches together is by joining without tacking a paper template to each patch. Put the template on the wrong side of the material and work around the shape with a fine pencil (Fig 8a). Mark a 1 cm seam allowance around each patch and cut out. Place the patches right sides together and pin along the matched drawn lines. Handsew along the pencil line with small regular running stitches taking the thread back two stitches for extra security at the end (Fig 8b). Press the seam allowance to one side, not open, for strength.

## Machine Patchwork

For machine patchwork, use firmly-woven fabrics such as dress-weight cotton or cotton polyester. Velvets, silks and fine wools are also suitable, but they are more difficult to handle. For conventional, functional quilts, use fabrics which will wash and are of the same weight. Changes in textures of fabrics are interesting to use for experimental work.

Cut out the required number of patches following the American method described. For greater accuracy in joining, cut and apply a template shape for each patch in medium-weight iron-on interfacing. This will give weight to the patchwork and make for easier machining (Fig 9a). With the right sides together, pin the patches in threes along the matched drawn lines. Place a pin at each corner first, and then pin at intervals along the line (Fig 9b). Machine the patches together using a No. 2 stitch, and cut the threads as you proceed. Press the seams open (Fig 9c).

To complete the patched square, pin the strips, right sides together, matching the seams exactly (Fig 9d). Machine the three strips together and press the seams to one side (Fig 9e). If using a light and a dark fabric together, press the seam towards the dark fabric. Cut all the threads. As an alternative to tacking, and to save valuable time, it is possible to machine over pins which have been put into the seams, at right angles to the edge, removing them when the patches are joined.

**Fig 8** The traditional American method of joining patches

**Fig 9** Machine patchwork

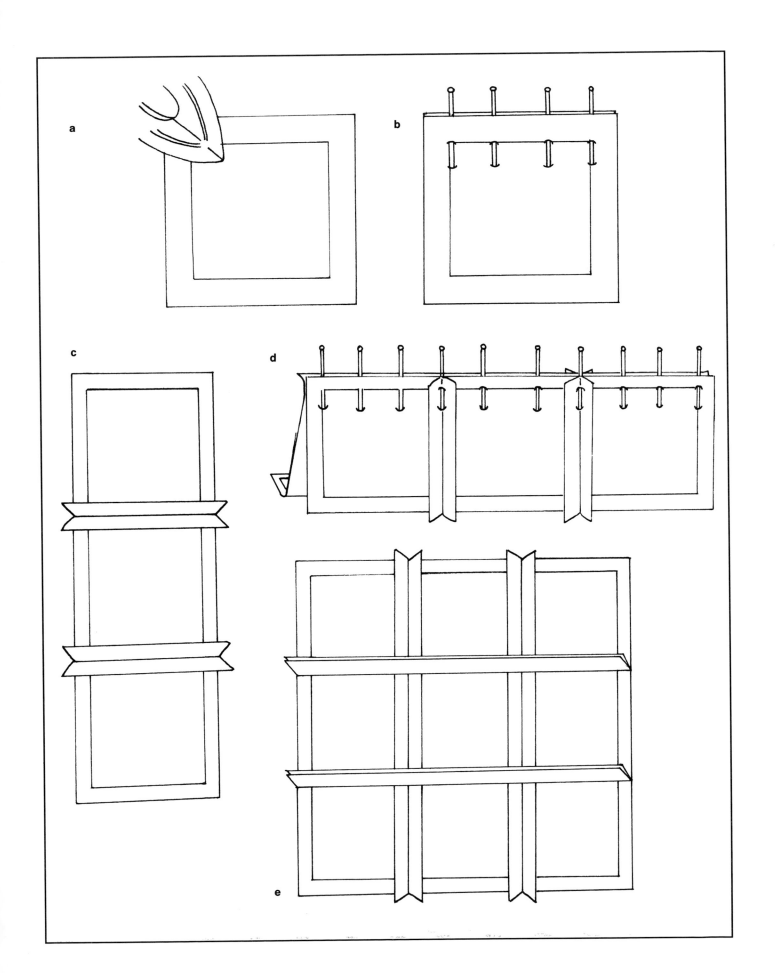

13

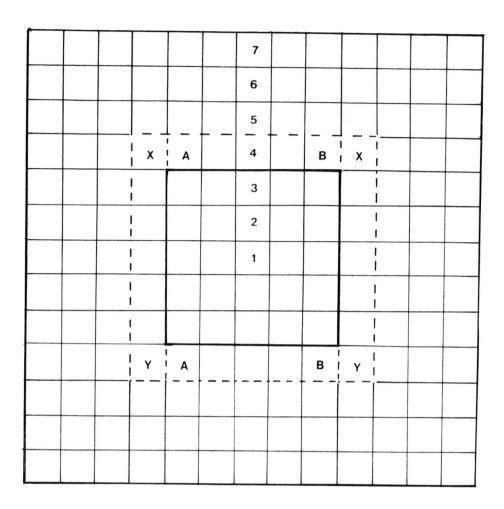

**Fig 10** Sewing a central patched square on a square quilt

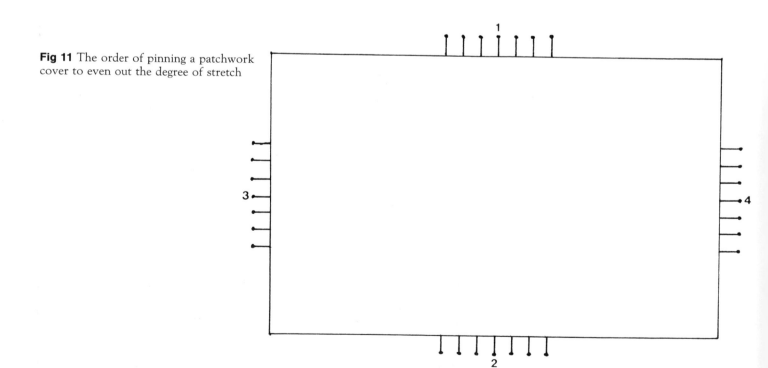

**Fig 11** The order of pinning a patchwork cover to even out the degree of stretch

14

For a rectangular quilt, make the required number of nine-patch units and join them into longer strips, finally machining together the long seams. To make a square quilt, sew a central patched square as shown (Fig 10). Continue to work in strips as follows; make two strips a–b and sew to the central square area. Then make two strips x–y, and sew to the sides of the central square. Continue adding strips in the sequence until the entire square is made up.

## Stretching the cover

Stretching is an embroidery technique which can be employed to improve the appearance of a finished patchwork piece and avoid unnecessary pressing. The work is dampened, and the stretcing process pulls out fine creases, which enables the piece to be pulled out to the correct finished size. It is carried out on a large cork-tiled surface or a cork tiled floor. Place an old blanket over the cork surface and dampen it with a water spray. Lay the finished patchwork over and dampen with the water spray until it is stretchy. Line up one edge of the work against a straight edge of the cork tiles, or about 6 cm from the edge of the board. Begin pinning this edge from the centre outwards, using drawing pins or special T-pins, which are available from educational suppliers. To even out the degree of stretch, pull the work and pin on the opposite side, 2, followed by side 3, and side 4. Place the pins evenly, approximately 3 cm apart until the work is pinned all round the edges (Fig 11). Readjust if necessary. Finish by respraying the work lightly. The work should be left until it is completely dry, which may take several hours or as long as overnight. Whilst the work is stretched, stray ends can be cut off and an inspection made for any faults.

## Backing the quilt

The quilt back can either be utilitarian or considered as an integral part of the statement the designer is expressing. Many of today's designers use the latter approach (Fig 12). Choose a similar weight and colour of material to that used for the top, and cut the back the same size as the front cover, including a seam allowance. Once the back is complete, decisions can be made about quilting.

## Marking out for quilting

To mark out the quilt design use a special fabric marking pen or a water soluble pencil in a pale colour which tones with the colours of the piece, so that any lines which show can later be removed with water and a paintbrush. Templates for quilting can be bought, or improvised using saucers, plates, biscuit cutters, etc. Long straight lines can be made with strips of masking tape which can be applied as a guide to sew against, and later peeled off.

## Wadding

Traditional fillings are still used as wadding, and cotton wadding gives a flat, gently padded surface which appeals to many quiltmakers. Cotton, however, must be closely quilted to keep the wadding evenly distributed, which is necessary if the quilt is to be washed. For this reason, polyester wadding is often used. Polyester is a puffier filling, available in different weights; a 2 oz filling per metre is thin and easy to sew through. If the wadding is too narrow for the quilt it can be seamed using a herringbone stitch to give a flat, even join.

**Fig 12** A quilt back design

### The quilt border

The quilt border needs to be considered in relation to the pattern and size of the finished top. Most borders are joined with straight edges at the corners or with a mitred seam. A simple and effective border can be made using contrasting or blending colours. Join two strips to each side of the quilt, allowing 1 cm for the seam. Join two longer strips at the top and bottom and press the seams to one side.

### Tacking

Spread the quilt backing on a large flat surface with the wrong side uppermost. Lay the quilt wadding over the quilt back, and finally cover both these with the quilt top, facing upwards. Smooth out any wrinkles and then pin, or tack, all the layers together, working from the centre outwards as shown in the diagram (Fig 13).

### Quilting

Using a quilting thread and a No. 9 between needle, thread the needle and knot one end. Draw the needle through the wadding and cover, bringing it up where the first stitch is to start. Tug gently to pull the knot into the wadding and secure the thread. Make small, straight, even running stitches through all three layers of the quilt. To finish off the stitching, take small stitches over the last quilting stitch, then draw the needle through the wadding layer and clip the thread, under tension, to pull the final stitch back into the quilt.

**Fig 13** Tacking the quilt top

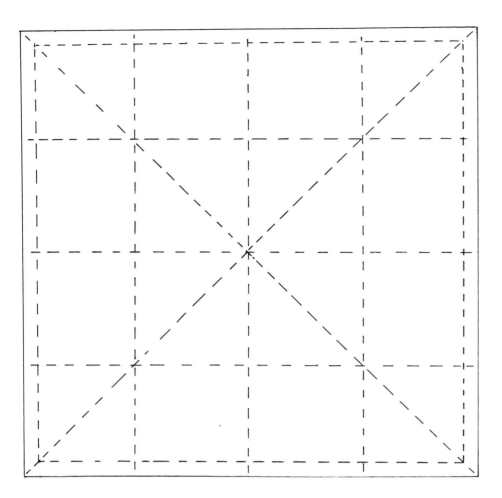

## Tie quilting or tufting

This is a quicker method of quilting, which can also be used as a decorative coloured and textured feature on either the front or back of the quilt. Different embroidery threads can be used, such as silks, cottons, wool and rayon. The ties can be made at joining points of the patchwork units, or as an additional form of decoration within the patched area (Fig 14). Using two thicknesses of thread, take a stab stitch through all the quilt layers (a). Pull the threads together, leaving a tail of about 6 cm (b). Tie the two ends firmly together with a reef knot, and snip to the required length (c).

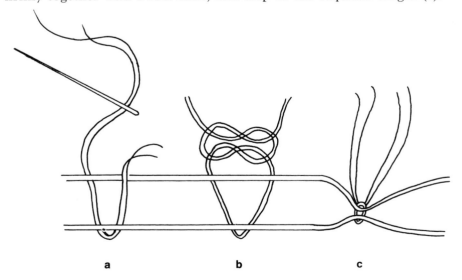

**Fig 14** Tie quilting          a                    b                    c

## Finishing

Cut the wadding layer to the correct size, turn the border over the edges of the back cover and mitre the corners (Fig 15), using a ladder stitch to secure them (Fig 16). Slip stitch the border to the back cover around the sides. The quilt may also be finished without a border by making the back to match the size of the top, turning in the seam allowance of the top and bottom inwards, and slip stitching them together round the sides.

**Fig 15** A mitred corner

**Fig 16** Ladder stitch

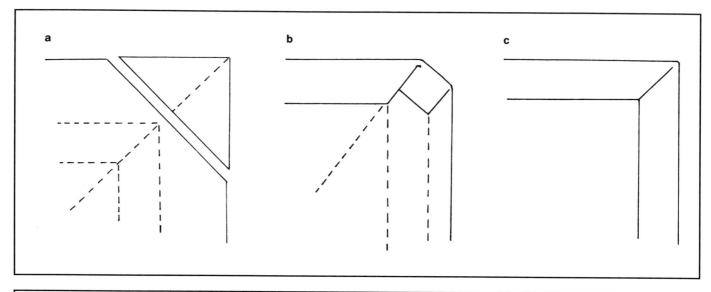

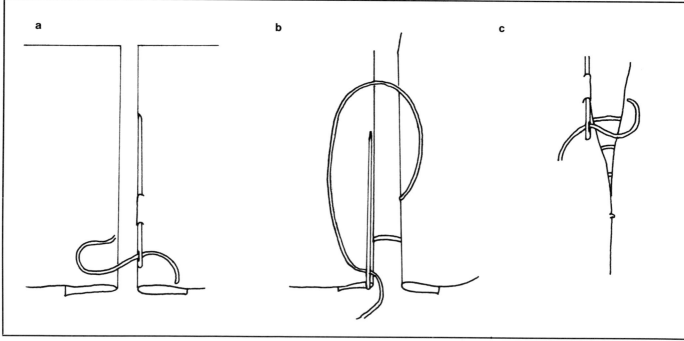

# Design: techniques
# and interpretation

**Fig 17** The tactile qualities of the quilt

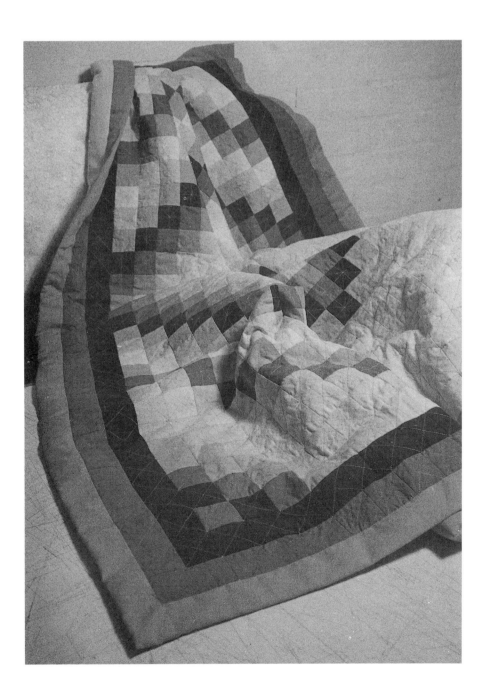

Experience of quiltmaking creates an awareness of the unique flexibility which the quilt allows. All the design elements of colour, shape, edge and texture are an intrinsic part of the quiltmaking process. Colour is not merely on the surface, as in easel art, it is in the fibre; shape is not merely outlined, it contours. The edges of fabric pieces can be felt and explored in a way that no drawn or painted shape can be. Pattern and design can be experienced from both front and back and generally manipulated in ways which could not be used if they were purely two-dimensional (Fig 17).

Because of all these considerations, it is not always necessary to have any starting point other than a collection of fabrics in various colours and textures of your choosing. Fabrics can be arranged on the floor or table, or, better still, pinned to a soft board in various combinations so that they give ideas for designs relating directly to fabric and thread which are an intrinsic part of textile art. From these experiments it is possible to relate shape to shape, edge to edge, and to note exciting and unusual combinations of colour and texture. A record can be kept by taking photographs of the various arrangements, or samples can be made and stored in a sketchbook (Fig 18).

**Fig 18** An experimental arrangement of fabric and threads. A useful way to try out ideas during the early stages of designing a quilt

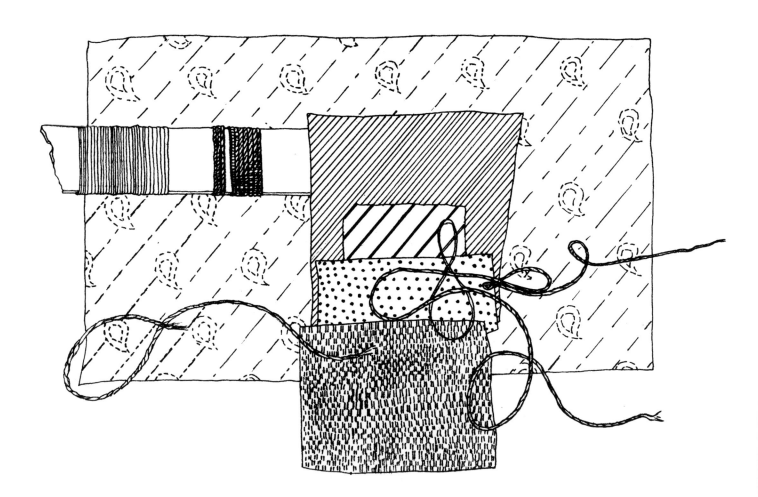

Working from a design source in addition to experimenting with abstract fabric and colour arrangements can enrich the activity of quilt designing. Design sources as wide as we want to make them, from traditional themes of flowers and plants, through still life and landscape. The human figure also offers great potential as a theme for quilts and many facets of human everyday activity can be portrayed representationally or in abstract ways (Figs 19–22).

It is important to remember that whenever you find a source of inspiration it is design you are looking for and not something to copy or imitate as closely and as representationally as possible. Patchwork and quilting are design media and the artists must choose and emphasise which elements of inspirational source they wish to use and then work out a design which has their own personal stamp on it.

Look at the inspirational source as a whole and try to decide what it is that appeals to you. Is it the delicacy of flowing rounded lines within an object? Is it clear cut geometrical pattern? Or maybe it is the general distribution of light and shade within a beautiful shape? Colour and texture may strike you as exciting, or the subject matter may have a strong emotional appeal relating to memories, experiences or dreams. You may have many reasons for wanting to use an idea, but by analysing its attractions you will probably be able to find those parts of the design which are most important to you. In this way those parts will be emphasised and the parts which are not as important to your mental design can be dispensed with. Drawing can help to explain and clarify your ideas at this stage. Drawing is the designer's way of exploring the design elements of line, tonal pattern, the distribution of shapes and colour, so that gradually the design gains emphasis in some areas and loses elements which are less important (Fig 23).

The next stage is to try out different interpretations using a variety of fabrics so that the idea is worked in fabric and thread. These sample pieces will often suggest design and technique ideas more readily than drawn and painted designs. Painted fabrics, patterned fabrics and combinations of both can be used and, because the design for a quilt does not need to represent any particular object you may choose to change the colour scheme or reduce all colour to monochrome. But think carefully about this and consider whether by changing the colour you may lose some essential part of the original design. Are the tonal values right or can they be made more exciting by exaggerating them. Perhaps colour can be dispensed with altogether and texture can become more important as a design element. In a quilt design colour changes may be emphasised subtly and it is important to link colour and tone to the surrounding shapes and border. Colour can therefore be used in a very personal way.

Experimental designing does not mean that workmanship is sacrificed; on the contrary all the quiltmakers featured in this book have stressed its importance in their own work. Beautiful stitchery, and meticulous quilt construction can be the prime concern of the quilt artist. The aim is to breathe life into a traditional idea and to create something tangible, unique and personal. By experimentation it is possible to build on experience and to design quilts which relate directly to your ideas (Figs 24–26).

**Figs 19 & 20** (overleaf) Working from a design source: a positive print developed from a photograph which was screen printed onto cotton lawn. Prints can be created on fabric using the photo screen printing process, which enables the artist to work directly from the design source instead of being limited to bought manufactured prints. The print illustrated is integrated into the quilt design shown on the front cover. Christine Nelson, 1987

Figs 21 & 22 Working from a design source: sketchbook pages showing a quilt design developed from photographs and paintings of buildings. Eiluned Edwards, 1987

**Fig 23** Sketchbook drawings for Liverpool Dockland 1987, Eiluned Edwards

**Fig 24** Working from a design source: a self portrait in coloured cotton fabrics. The patchwork panel design is taken from a video image sequence. Joe Boyle, 1987

**Fig 25** Detail of a quilt in plain and shot silk fabrics, bonded to a backing fabric, and machine embroidered. Andrea Fothergill, 1984

**Fig 26** Designing a quilt: a working drawing. Isabel Dibden-Wright

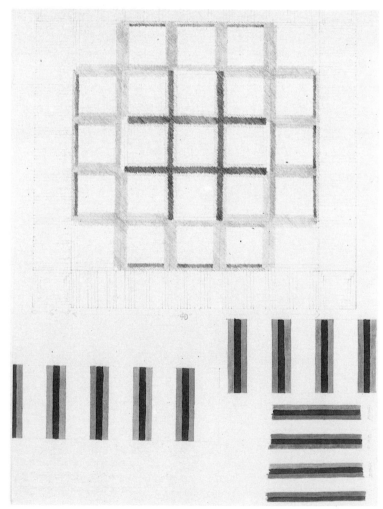

**Fig 27** Patchwork sampling: a log cabin patchwork sample with inset photograph. Christine Nelson, 1987

**Fig 28** Patchwork sampling: a cathedral window patchwork sample in black and white fabrics of varying textures. Isabel Dibden-Wright

# Progress through technique

The progress of one artist quiltmaker reveals how she has related and developed her technique to fit her artistic interests. After completing a Diploma course in Fashion and Textiles at St Martin's College of Art in London, Pauline Burbidge worked in the fashion business for four years, but became disillusioned with the fashion world and tired of adapting designs to fit the human body. Quiltmaking presented itself as an attractive alternative, allowing her to continue to deal with fabric and colour in a more basic way.

Her first quilts were designed and made to traditional American block forms, using as a guide the book *Patchwork Quilts, and the Women who made them* by Ruth Finley. Making her first quilt satisfied her need to work in a flat format, and opened up endless possibilities for her artistic skills to develop. For two years she survived by working as a freelance pattern-cutter for half the week, spending the rest of her time on her patchwork. She advertised in *Crafts* magazine, ran workshops in a hired room to teach patchwork, wrote a book *Patchwork for Pleasure and Profit*, and obtained a setting-up grant from the Crafts Council.

Foyles Bookshop Art Gallery was the venue for the artist's first exhibition of quilts, where one piece of work was sold and a second piece was commissioned. Two years of hard work followed, leading to several successful commissions, and eventually to her now international reputation as a quiltmaker. The craftsmanship in Pauline Burbidge's quilts is meticulous and she is excited by considerations of scale, small to large, and by the translation of idea to paper, and then into fabric. She combines traditional methods of quiltmaking with personal imagery which relates positively to contemporary ideas.

Her work can be divided into periods. From 1975–80 she used pictorial, figurative imagery as her inspiration. One of her first quilts was *Korky the Cat*, produced in 1975 (Fig 29). In this, the design is made up of squares, giving the effect of a computer printout. This was followed by a number of quilts using traditional American motifs, such as fruit baskets and maple leaves, which she began to incorporate using a strip method of construction instead of squares.

The idea of using small pieces of fabric to make a pictorial jigsaw in a quilt called *Large Fruit Basket* (1979) was a breakthrough (Fig 30). From this, Pauline Burbidge progressed to dyeing her own fabrics, and through this process gained greater control over the work she produced. She used strips instead of joining rows of squares together. Basically the strip is all one piece until the colour changes, at which point there is a seam. To make up

**Fig 29** *Korky the Cat* (1977) 96″ × 106″, Pauline Burbidge

the quilt, the rows are joined. This method is useful when a high degree of detail is required.

Designing on her own themes followed, and from 1977–81 she explored traditional techniques in her own way. Some of this work was on an Egyptian theme, arising from an idea which came from a client. After spending time making preparatory drawings in the Egyptian section of the British Museum, she produced several designs on this theme and devised her own system of effective block-making. Beginning with a drawing of the design on graph paper, she works out the grid of straight lines through the design and draws it up to scale to obtain a good impression of the finished image. This initial paper design acts as a reference point for the specific shapes and colours planned. She usually makes a line drawing first and, when satisfied, uses crayons to show colour. Any changes can be made at this point, before committing the idea to cloth.

When the block is drawn out to size on tracing paper, each piece is numbered and these numbers transferred to the graph paper drawing for cross-reference. The shapes are then cut out, pasted down on card, and a seam allowance of 6 mm added on all sides. These shapes are then used as templates to draw on the fabric before cutting into patches. The patchwork pieces are put together one step at a time and are then joined into larger sections.

Pauline Burbidge's interest in the way the kaleidoscope breaks up images

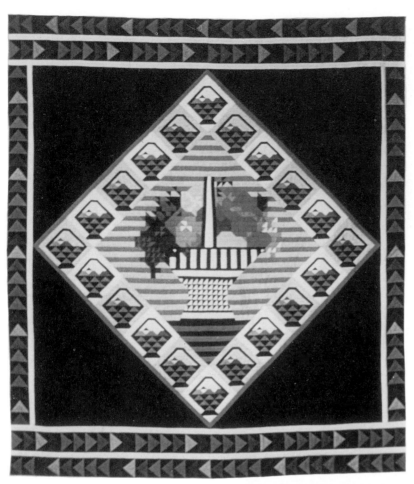

**Fig 30** *Large Fruit Basket* (1979) 82″ × 92″, Pauline Burbidge

**Fig 31** *Cubic Log Cabin* (1982) 71″ × 66″, Pauline Burbidge

into pattern led her to develop a series of quilts inspired by kaleidoscope patterns. She used a kaleidoscope which was empty and clear, without any beads or coloured shapes, and simply produced eight clear images reflecting from the mirrors. By fixing the kaleidoscope into position, she had both hands free to draw things she saw through it, coming up with a myriad of design possibilities.

The kaleidoscope design manipulations of flat pattern were integrated into quilts produced from 1980–83, where three-dimensional illusion became a design theme, produced as a result of these experiments. Much of this work was carried out in Honan silk, used because of its excellent handling quality and weight. Pauline Burbidge began to use this fabric in 1980, finding its vibrant colour appropriate to her ideas, and continues to use this material, combined with a thin cotton wadding and backing fabric, stitching all three layers together by machine. A quilt produced during this time, *Cubic Log Cabin Quilt*, won an award at the American Quilt National Exhibition in 1983 (Fig 31).

Recent work since 1986 has been influenced by her links with industry through a project organised by Nottingham Castle Museum which is named 'The Artist in Industry'. This gave her the opportunity to work in a commercial quilting factory in Nottingham which, in turn, led to the creation of more pieces. She was able to use an industrial quilting machine, and to explore design ideas further, as well as speeding up the process of making. Some of the quilts and cushions produced on the industrial machine are simple, stark and austere designs with limited colour.

Alongside this development, Pauline Burbidge has also made a series of paper collages on a still life theme which contrast with the hard-edged geometric designs she has produced. Torn paper studies are her starting point. The use of pattern in her choice of subject, together with patterns formed by the repeated unit, plays a significant role in the finished design of this work. She finds this way of working very exciting and feels it is just the beginning of a long exploration of working this theme. *The Pink Teapot* (colour plate) quilt she has produced shows her artistic progression. It is concerned with fluid images, yet it retains the strength of fine and rigid stitchery which the industrial quilting machine gives it.

In studying Pauline Burbidge's work the viewer is struck by the way she has used her skills as a cutter to develop her technique. The problem-solving involved in her designing integrates successfully with her chosen themes in the finished work.

# The quilt surface

When artists are directly involved with the surface qualities of fabric, in searching for insight into how it can be manipulated and changed through experimental processes, they produce work of an amazing variety which ranges from the subtle to the strident. Deirdre Amsden, Christine Mitchell and Esther Barrett approach quiltmaking through a variety of methods and techniques, but all are concerned with the surface, tone, and qualities of edge they achieve in their finished work.

Deirdre Amsden's delicate colour-wash studies are a recurring theme in which small patches are graded into washes of colour and further blended

**Fig 32** *Colourwash Stripe II* (1986) *22″ × 22″*, Dierdre Amsden

*Stitched stripes* (1980) 36″ × 48″, Esther
Barrett

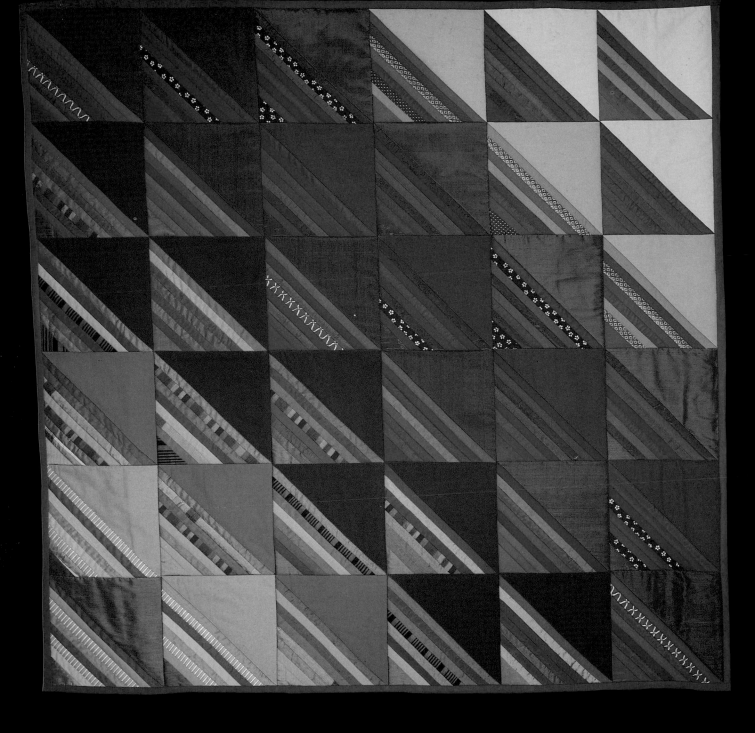

*Symit* (1987), Isabel Dibden-Wright

*Arched Trellis* (1983) 32″ × 48″, Andrea
Fothergill

*Still Life IV* (1985) 54″ × 60″, Christine
Mitchell

**Fig 33** *Colourwash Cubes* (1987) 72″ × 69″, Dierdre Amsden

and textured with quilting patterns, creating very subtle changes of surface and edge. The tonal arrangement is, however, clearly readable, yet the carefully modulated surface invites close observation, appreciation, and belies the simplicity of the technique (Fig 32).

The artist studied at Cambridge School of Art as an illustrator, and, after working in this field for a number of years, taught herself quilting and began making quilts in 1976. Her interest in cutting and rearranging fabrics was aroused when she was given a sample book of furnishing fabrics, and, in an attempt to obtain patches to make into a design, cut up the large patterned fabrics into small squares and sorted them into tones – dark, medium dark, medium light and light – which she then arranged into a diamond formation shading from a light centre, through to dark, and back to light, and so on.

Several years later, when using Liberty 'Tana' lawn off-cuts for a crib quilt, she once again cut small squares and, choosing one of each fabric, shaded them into a wash of colour from dark at the top down to light. This led to the first series of small hangings, all on simple shading themes. Later, when she returned to this colour-wash concept, it was to explore tonal contrasts as well as shading. The next series of hangings were striped, quartered diagonally or framed. In turn, these explorations led to work relating to the illusion of transparency, where one layer appeared to overlap another. All these pieces were small, their size being related to the number of Liberty lawn fabrics to hand. Recently, the artist has utilised a greater variety of fabric and patterns, resulting in larger scale pieces with a richer stippled effect (Fig 33).

Through her working method Deirdre Amsden disguises the patchwork seaming to create a whole colour field effect which visually allies her work

**Fig 34** *Still Life II* (1985) 72" × 48", Christine Mitchell

to painted surfaces, as though washes of colour have been applied and blended. She cuts more patches than she needs, laying them out in rows according to tone. She works from rough pencil sketches which indicate tonal contrasts and shading only: the colour placement and finished size of the piece evolves (as does the overall design sometimes) whilst arranging the fabric patches. Arranging the patches is like doing a jigsaw puzzle, and finding the right place for each patch in relation to those around it is a fascinating design problem. An artist's reducing glass helps in judging whether the tones and colours of the patches blend well before they are sewn together. The seams of the patchwork are mostly pressed open to keep them as flat and unobtrusive as possible, so that the work resembles a whole piece of cloth. Hand quilting further disguises the seaming construction and adds texture. This exploration of tone and texture through patchwork and quilting is of continuing interest to Deirdre Amsden.

Her work is rooted in the English style of patchwork, yet links with French Post-Impressionist painting by nature of the effect of shimmering broken light, created by the myriad of patterned fabrics she uses.

In contrast, Christine Mitchell originates quilt surfaces which are rumbustuous and in striking relief, inspired by fragmented images and distorted patterns. She trained as a designer of carpets and related textiles at Kidderminster College of Further Education and her interest in patchwork is a recent development. She creates large-scale quilts, and patches together fabrics which are folded, scrumpled or shirred (Fig 34). Parts of the surface are also dealt with more formally, integrating carefully pleated areas. This active surface is created from fabric which is painted upon, using vigorous strokes and stippling, from representations of still life groups, broken glass

and china, and torn and crumpled papers. The changes in the edge of the patched textiles is sometimes emphasised by a change of form, and at other times ignored, resulting in a statement of spatial ambiguity. The colours Christine Mitchell uses have a Fauvist exuberance, and her work shows energy and complex changes of scale.

An artist whose work is characterised by her experimental approach to traditional techniques is Esther Barrett, and this, she says, 'Is why some people don't particularly like my work, because I bend the rules or ignore what is considered to be right.' It is these features, however, that make her work exciting and innovative. She has developed techniques using the reverse side of patchwork, creating new surface patterns by retaining paper templates in the finished work. She is also interested in the textural interest which can be exploited by stitchery on paper in combination with fabric (Fig 35).

Born in Gloucestershire, Esther Barrett was trained as a designer at Loughborough College of Art and Design where she gained a BA(Hons) degree in Textiles/Fashion. All aspects of quilting and patchwork excite her – colour and pattern are probably top of the list, but it also includes the tactile quality of quilts and their dual role of practicality as bed coverings and as works of art. She is also motivated by the versatility of the design work which the actual making involves. Stitching seam after seam to make a large quilt out of a pile of bits, and mixing and matching of fabrics, are both processes which relate to her work as a textile designer. Her passion for patchwork was formed when she saw her first quilt exhibition whilst still at school, and she was amazed by the variety and the possibilities patchwork afforded. Her first attempts were very traditional, using as a guide Averil Colby's patchwork book, which gave her a good, basic

**Fig 36** *Stitched Stripes* (1980) (detail), 36″ × 48″, Esther Barrett

understanding of techniques. Traditional patchwork remains an important source of inspiration, but her own ideas have developed through a more thorough exploration of the medium whilst she studied at art college.

All her techniques are adaptations, in different ways, of traditional patchwork ideas. For instance, the technique is based upon template patchwork, but instead of taking the papers out of the work when it has been stitched together, she retains them and uses the front of the quilt as the back. The raw edges of the patchwork are included on the right side of the work as part of the design. *Stitched Stripes* (1980) is a wall-hanging which uses this technique (Fig 36). It was produced during her final year at art college, as a result of spending some time exploring various patchwork techniques, particularly the use of the reverse side of template patchwork. The overall design was influenced by the American method of using repeated blocks, each block being twelve inches square with a four-inch square in each centre. The whole hanging is richly decorated with pattern and colour, and both hand and machine stitching are employed in combination with paper and a variety of fabric and fibre types.

# 7

# The creative response to design ideas

Patchwork and quilting have always related directly to the type of design imagery which currently inspires Andrea Fothergill.

The necessity for technique is born out of these ideas. Her excitement in the technical processes and the skills she uses experimentally to extend her artistic vocabulary give rise to a greater range of personal expression.

The artist studied at Loughborough College of Art and Design,

**Fig 37** *Deckchair Canvas Quilt* (1973) 72" × 96", Andrea Fothergill

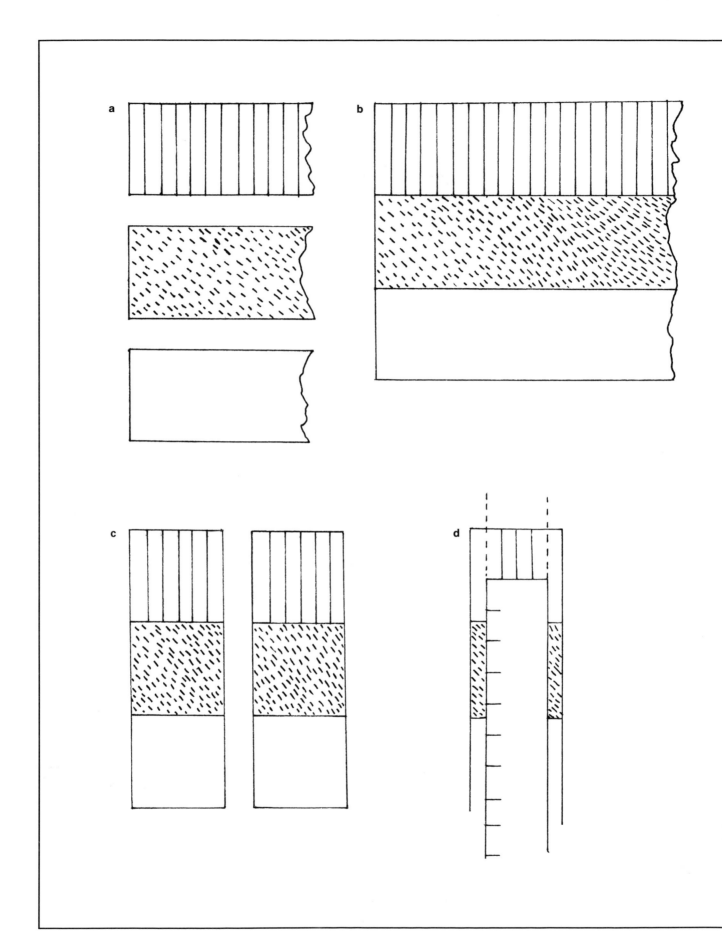

**Fig 38** Seminole piecing methods

e

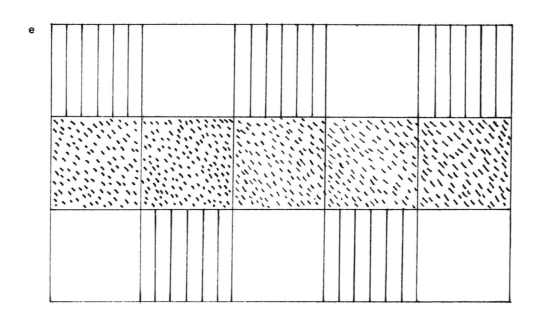

f

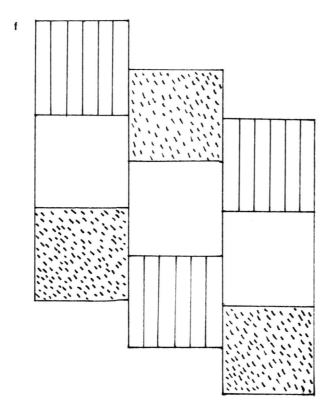

obtaining her BA(Hons) in Embroidery. On this course, patchwork was offered as one of a range of techniques, and it aroused Andrea Fothergill's interest, encouraging her, through a process of self-discovery, to work some of the traditional techniques as samples. This led to the realisation that patchwork was most satisfactory when consideration was given to the tonal values and repeat elements. She produced a large quilt, experimenting with the log cabin technique using deckchair canvas and cotton voile material (Fig 37). Her interest in piecing and patchwork techniques progressed further after seeing a tiny scrap of North American pieced leather-craft work. Inspired by this, she devised her own method of patchwork, based upon Seminole piecing used by the North American Indians.

## Seminole patchwork

Seminole patchwork differs from most American patchwork in its construction as well as its appearance. It is made by sewing torn strips of fabric together to form long multicoloured bands. The bands are then cut into segments which are arranged and joined together in geometric designs.

The Seminole Indians used new fabric to make patchwork for clothing which was pieced but not quilted. Their designs use geometric repetition and bring a unique precision to the cut and joined band process. In general they chose bright colours and used colour combinations of vibrance that would have shocked the conservative colonists, whose fashion in patchwork at that time was for restrained colour. The Indians often set clear, bright colours against black.

## A simple method of seminole piecing

First experiments can be made with one band made up of three single strips that are only a few inches wide, cut from the full width of the fabric. Choose one light, one medium and one dark toned fabric. To make a straight cut pattern, tear or cut three stripes of fabric (Fig 38a) and join them lengthwise by machine (Fig 38b). Cut ten segments of equal size, and stack them in the order in which they will be joined (Fig 38c). Mark seam lines from an adjacent parallel seam to ensure exact alignment (Fig 38d). Join five strips evenly with the top and bottom in alternative positions (Fig 38e). Simple unit strips can be made from the same band. Sizes of the segments in these examples vary, and show possibilities of patterns from one simple piecing.

Another technique which Andrea Fothergill has developed in her work is that of bonding one fabric to another. This method has developed from one of the first known methods of applying fabrics, known as appliqué.

## Appliqué and bonding techniques

Appliqué is the technique of applying pieces of fabric to a background by securing turned-in raw edges with small stitches. For the quiltmaker it offers a method of creating freer and curvilinear designs which can be more naturalistic than block piecing. Designs can be symmetrical and cut from folded paper, or asymmetrical and drawn freehand.

Draw the design, cut it out, and paste on cardboard to form a template. Place the template on the right side of your fabric, and draw around the shape with a water-soluble pencil, using a light colour on dark fabrics and a dark colour on light fabrics. Cut out the appliqué shape with a 6 mm seam allowance if the edges are to be handstitched down. Turn in the seam allowance, pin and then slip-stitch the shape into place.

Many of today's quilt artists use adhesive to apply appliqué shapes to the backing fabric. This gives greater freedom of expression by allowing more complex shapes of fabric and paper to be pieced, or layered, together

**Fig 39** A patchwork appliqué sample using 'Bondaweb', Andrea Fothergill

(Fig 39). For this method the appliqué shapes are attached to a Bondaweb backing. Bondaweb is a paper-backed adhesive which is used to bond materials together using a dry domestic iron. Place the Bondaweb adhesive side downwards on the wrong side of the fabric. The design is then drawn in reverse on the paper backing. Iron the Bondaweb and the fabric layer together with a hot, dry iron and leave to cool. Cut out the drawn design shape, and peel off the paper, leaving an adhesive layer on the fabric. Place the fabric motif, with its now fused adhesive, into position on the main fabric. Cover with a damp cloth, press with a steam iron and leave the bonded fabrics to cool. The edges can either be left raw, or stitchery, such as a machine satin stitch, applied.

Andrea Fothergill has made a quilt, *Arched Trellis*, using these two techniques. The design is formed from baskets of flowers and garden borders, and is the result of much experiment to find satisfactory piecing and composition techniques. The techniques have made it possible to freely combine shapes, colours and fabrics. The additional use of stitchery and quilting give greater impact to the intricacies of the design (Figs 40 and 41).

The difficulties involved in combining these techniques were challeng-ing, and were overcome by a great deal of sampling. Experiments involving composition, colour, tone and scale were made to achieve the most satisfying result. Andrea Fothergill considers that this method of designing and making is essential, because a paper design, however well painted or drawn, does not accurately reflect the finished embroidery. She does draw and design on paper, however, often using graph paper for accurate

**Fig 40** Detail of *Arched Trellis* (1983) showing Seminole band bonding techniques, Andrea Fothergill

**Fig 41** Detail of *Arched Trellis* (1983)

measurement, scaling, and to establish simple tonal values, before committing her ideas to cloth.

She enjoys collecting fabrics and is constantly seeking new and unusual ones to add to the large collection which is carefully stored in the studio. Very little is wasted, and even tiny scraps are kept in polythene bags and often displayed to act as a stimulus for new ideas or for experiments.

Important considerations are thread and stitch qualities, whether using hand or machine methods. Stitch quality is seen as a pictorial device to modify shapes, edge, colour, line or texture. Equally important is the aesthetic enjoyment of the medium itself: the rich variety of thread manipulations which creates a surface unique to embroidery. Control of colour and tone is seen as vital and Andra Fothergill has a full understanding of how colour works. Harmony, discord and proportion of colour, as well as control of tonal values, play an important part in her work.

An influential teacher, first at Loughborough, and now at Birmingham Polytechnic, Andrea Fothergill readily communicates her enthusiasm for her experimental approach to patchwork, quilting and embroidery. She uses a simple rather than an obscure art language, and stresses that to be successful a piece 'must work', meaning that all the elements must come together to create a satisfying whole. There is a tendency to deal with the areas within a piece of work without relating them to the whole. A piece works when the overall impression is of organised unity, and the viewer is aware of a total integration of all elements. To achieve this totality in her own work, the artist tends to work in small areas first, bringing them together to make a larger piece. Throughout this process she is prepared to change the design frequently in order to achieve a satisfying whole.

Whilst it is possible to respond to technique in a creative way, Andrea Fothergill's work is usually conceived the other way around. Although she is excited by technical processes, she sees them as skills which can extend her capacity to work freely with her ideas.

Changes in her work occur as an idea becomes exhausted, and there is a natural progression of experiments leading from one idea to another. She finds it possible to work in a variety of ways, and does not have preferences. The scale, materials, and techniques that she uses arise as a result of careful research and analysis of source material. The scale of her current work is small: a series of embroideries inspired by ancient Peruvian textiles. She is combining hand knitting with embroidery in a narrative, slightly humorous form. This project uses powerful colour combinations and a rich mix of knitting, sewing and appliqué on a shot tussah silk background.

Andrea Fothergill enjoys a challenge, rather than an undemanding routine, and is constantly striving to achieve a unique personal quality in her work.

Eiluned Edwards is an artist who has recently obtained a BA(Hons) degree in Textiles at Trent Polytechnic, Nottingham. She also uses technique as an experimental springboard for piecing ideas.

During the summer of 1986, a visit to the United States evoked a strong interest in Amish and Mennonite quilts. Travelling to Mexico towards the end of her visit, she was impressed by Mexican design, particularly Mayan architecture. Her liking for patterns and harmonies which she could observe and draw, and her response to structure, led her to produce designs for pieces inspired by the Liverpool Docks. In this work she evokes a sense of place, using adaptations of traditional quilting methods and batik dyeing. Her sketchbook drawings and watercolours are an important art language tool in relation to the finished piece. She is happiest with her drawing when it is spontaneous and unlaboured, directly reflecting her feelings for the subject.

**Fig 42** Traditional Mola reverse appliqué technique with folded and secured edges

**Fig 43** Traditional Mola reverse appliqué technique with slashed and frayed edges

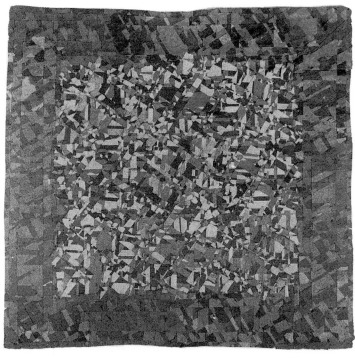

Fig 44 Technique sample, Eiluned Edwards

Fig 45 *Crazy 1*, 54″ × 54″, Eiluned Edwards

She uses plain white, medium weight cotton fabric which is dyed a base colour using Dylon or Procion dye. Domestic bleach is then spattered on some of the fabric, encouraging accidental effects and damage to the fabric fibres which echo the weathering of the girders on which she is basing her design. The fabric is then rinsed out and dried.

Eilund Edwards has adapted a piecing technique which is based upon Mola reverse appliqué, also known as Mola work, which was skilfully practised by Kuna Indian women of the San Blas Islands off the coast of Panama. Layers of fabric, usually four, are cut away revealing the material below. The layers can either be folded and secured with tiny hem stitches (Fig 42) or slashed and frayed for a textural effect (Fig 43).

So that the work is a manageable size to sew, the artist works with one yard-square piece of fabric and, after the dyeing process, coats both sides of the fabric with batik wax using a large decorating brush. The fabric is then screwed up to achieve a variety of breakage in the wax and then re-dyed; the whole process can be carried out easily at home. The particular appeal of textiles to the artist lies in its accessibility; textiles of one sort or another are in daily usage and a feature of everyone's life.

After dyeing, the wax is ironed out on newsprint, leaving the fabric slightly stiffened. It is then cut into strips and pieced in layers. These are joined, spontaneous horizontal cuts made, and the pieces joined into a patchwork on the sewing machine, using a straight stitch. Sometimes holes are punched, which relate to the rivets holding the girders in place; when four patchwork units have been produced, these are joined together with machine stitching to form a larger piece (Fig 44).

In the patchworks, both the front and the back relate to the artist's conceived ideas, beyond her immediate interpretation of layers of fabric inspired by building structures. The laminating process allows her to develop greater expression of her ideas. She is interested in art therapy and exploring the relationship between different areas of the brain and creative/expressive potential. The right side of the brain is the pattern-maker; the left acts as controller. The patchwork pieces are a vehicle for these ideas. The artist sees both back and front of the work as important, as each gives layers of meaning to the viewer. She does not, however, aim to control or change the back of the cloth layers; when she recognised this was happening, she allowed the back of the pieces to occur spontaneously, so that both accident and control contribute to the finished result (Fig 45).

Eiluned Edwards enjoys the work of artist/writers such as William Blake and Mervyn Peake, and also the paintings of Turner and Diego Rivera. Colin Wilson's books *The Outsider* and *Access to Inner Worlds*, together with work by Alice Miller, have influenced the content of her work. The artist considers that the best work is rarely produced without considerable effort and that it is important to try and drag the very most from oneself, to make a statement that has both coherence and integrity.

# Building on the traditional

Patterns are one of the ways we invest our ideas with order. A number of artists mention their enjoyment of arranging patterns, likening the design and making process of quilts to piecing a jigsaw. They also enjoy the rhythmic and pliable pattern possibilities quiltmaking affords, allowing for arrangements that can be formal or disorganised, but still remain related in terms of scale. The patterns from daily domestic life which played an important part in the patterning and design of traditional American patchwork quilts demonstrate a wealth of invention (Fig 46). These quilts show a lively approach to quiltmaking, and have a direct appeal, both in

**Fig 46** A traditional American quilt design

**Fig 47** *Iced Fancies* (1985) 48″ × 64″, Liz
Bruce

**Fig 48** *Fish on a Dish* (1985) 62″ × 48″,
Liz Bruce

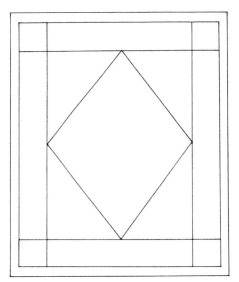

**Fig 49** A traditional Amish quilt design

terms of imagery, and in the bold shapes and simple tonal contrasts used.

Work by Liz Bruce relates to these traditions, but she draws her ideas from many sources, and simplifies images into patchwork blocks using bright cotton fabrics. Her work is mainly based upon still life compositions and collections of ephemera expressing her interest in the vernacular imagery of the twentieth century; they are often ironic comments on both the way we live now and the way we once lived (Fig 47). The patterns she evolves are informally arranged in areas across the quilt, giving large focal points of interest within a geometric framework. The quilts are direct in their appeal, and the surface quality is secondary to the impact of strong two-dimensional pattern. Liz Bruce trained as a painter at Exeter College of Art and undertook postgraduate studies in Textile Design at Leeds University, which led to her present position lecturing in printed textile and surface design at Southwark College, London. She has recently decided to devote most of her time to quiltmaking.

The link between an artist's native culture and techniques of working is often inherent. A Thai artist living and working in Britain, Siripan Kidd, creates quilts using Thai silks, and, through the medium of quiltmaking, communicates messages about her cultural background. A trained language teacher, she settled in this country and first became interested in patchwork as a medium through seeing a piece in a Leeds museum. This meticulous work, consisting of hand-pieced hexagons and using the English method, excited her interest in making a quilt and she proceeded to learn basic techniques.

During this time she also developed an interest in Amish quilts and produced some work from their patterns. Amish quilts are American in origin. The Amish people are descendants of European settlers who came to America around 1727, after breaking away from the Swiss religious Mennonite movement in 1693, and who settled on the fertile farmland of Pennsylvania. As their numbers grew, they divided into groups and in the early nineteenth century many moved further west to Ohio and Indiana. The most traditional Amish avoid any dependence on the outside world, rejecting the trappings of the twentieth century such as cars, telephones, electricity and modern clothes. Their textiles have always been plain and utilitarian, patterned fabrics being considered frivolous. Despite this austere approach, their quilts are often surprisingly bright, with striking unusual tonal colour effects which have been linked to modern abstract painting movements because of their direct simplicity. They are pieced from large, straight-edged pieces of cloth, and the quilting is worked in fine and elaborate patterns.

There are some general characteristics of Pennsylvanian Amish quilts which are considered typical in design. These include square shape and the design developed from the centre out towards the edges. Amish designs are often surrounded by wide borders edged with narrow binding, and are composed of one overall design, rather than a block pattern (Fig 49).

Siripan Kidd has incorporated some of these Amish characteristics in her work through the use of large plain areas, but gradually the piecing, the fabrics used and the context of her designs have been related to her own culture. Her recent pieces are very different from Amish work. She feels more comfortable working with strong colours, using silk. In Thailand, to wear bright colours is to be associated with the peasants and poorly educated: the sophisticated and educated choose muted Western colours for their clothes. In her native Thailand she loved strong colours, but was not allowed to wear them: now she has the freedom to express in her work the colours she missed when she was young.

Her design ideas have developed through drawing the shapes, designs and collections of forms that she remembers from home. Gradually, she has evolved ideas which relate to the roofs of the temples, the temple bells, the gold leaf from Buddha statues, the dark shiny greens of palm leaves, the saffron robes of the monks and the paddy fields. She has particularly tried to reproduce interpretations of the rain and puddles. She enjoys working with contrasts, either in colour or design, enjoying the tension this produces.

She thinks that it is important to present ideas of the present day telling the history of our own time, rather than just reproducing traditional patterns and designs. Her method of working is planned and methodical: she looks at the colours first, and when these suggest a theme to her, she sketches out a rough design. This is drawn out accurately on graph paper, and then enlarged to a suitable scale to decide the colour arrangement. She draws out the entire quilt to full size and then cuts it up, using the paper shapes as templates to draw round on the fabric. The fabric pieces are sewn

**Fig 50** *Temple* (1986) 45″ × 60″, Siripan Kidd

by hand, using the American method of joining. The quilting design is adjusted and changed as the work progresses, and if it is not successful she takes the stitching out and replaces it.

She has found the inspiration of developing and exploring her own design ideas a great challenge. She has produced three pieces using her own design based on a lotus flower, following with two pieces on the same theme but which had a more abstract quality. These pieces made her feel much freer and ready to break away from the purely traditional. Just as she wants to communicate traditions about her native land, however, she also wants to use the traditional craftsmanship of piecing and quilting as a way of putting her designs together (Fig 50).

The experience of love of other cultures, and conveying a message through traditional patchwork and quilting techniques, can also be the motivation for more reflective pieces. Isabel Dibden-Wright, who works within a framework of embroidery and design artistry, was influenced in her work by a period of time spent in the Far East during the early 1960s, when her father's job sent him to Singapore for three years. To go to such a different environment after spending her early childhood growing up in a tiny village in South Wales was an enormous change of lifestyle.

A fascination with the Far East began then, and she still feels a great empathy with South-East Asia, which is reflected in her work. Direct influences are the wonderful vibrant colours of the tropics, the stunning combination of colours made possible by the qualities of the light and heat, and the abundant plant life. Colours also reflect the cosmopolitan society of Singapore: races as diverse as Chinese, Malays, Indonesians, Indians from different parts of the sub-Continent, Japanese, Europeans, Americans and Australians are mixed in this tiny country.

It was in this multi-cultural society that the artist first became aware of fabric, particularly rich fabrics. Designing her own clothes, which were made up by dressmakers, gave her access to, and information on, the exotic fabrics which were available, from Malayan handwoven cotton to Thai raw silks. She particularly remembers from this time a beautiful blue Malayan fabric woven with a real silver weft.

This love of fabrics and colours found expression when she trained at Loughborough College of Art and Design, gaining her BA(Hons) in Embroidery. Influenced by an exhibition of North American quilts at a textile gallery in London and by quilting work other students were producing, she became involved in making quilts. An expert embroiderer, Isabel Dibden-Wright is much influenced by traditional methods. Among those she has employed are: Suffolk puffs, crazy patchwork, cathedral window piecing and log cabin patchwork. She considers fabrics and the geometric nature of patterns to be her major sources of inspiration when making quilts. Variety in ways of working fascinates her, and she is always delighted to find something she has not seen or read about before.

## A variety of patchwork methods: Suffolk puffs

Suffolk puffs are gathered, circular patches of fabric which are handsewn together with the edges touching, leaving small spaces in between. The most effective fabrics to use are fine ones, such as lightweight silk, soft cotton voile or cotton organdie. For a decorative panel, some plastics and nylon nets can give interesting results. The gathered side of the circle is placed to the front, and the central hole creates a decorative textural effect. This technique can be varied by using different sizes of circles, or by placing a decorative filling, such as scraps of fabric or threads, in transparent puffs. The gathering thread can also be left loose to reveal more of the inside which can be padded, or filled with a toning or contrasting colour.

Cut circles of fabric of twice the diameter of the required finished piece. Fold over a 6 mm turning to the wrong side and, using a strongly knotted thread, gather all around the edge (Fig 51a). Pull up the gathering thread as required and secure firmly. Flatten each shape so that the gathered area is centred (Fig 51b). Attach the puffs together using small back stitches at intervals around the circle (Fig 51c).

**Fig 51** Suffolk puffs patchwork technique

a

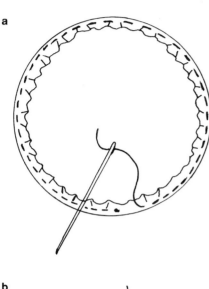

b

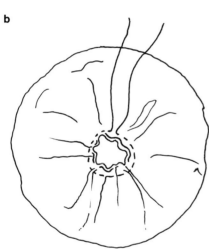

c

## Cathedral window

Begin by cutting sufficient squares of plain coloured fabric about twice the size of the finished square (16 cm). Make a 6 mm turning all round and hem in place (Fig 52a). Fold the four corners to the middle and press flat. Pin to secure (Fig 52b). Repeat, folding the corners of the smaller square to the middle and press flat (Fig 52c). Stitch the corners at the middle to form a diamond shape (Fig 52d). Stitch the squares together along the side. Cut out small squares of contrasting fabric 6 mm smaller than the diamond formed between the two squares. Pin the fabric on top of the seam between the joined squares (Fig 52e). Turn the folded edges of the squares over the fabric patch and stab stitch through all layers of fabric (Fig 52f).

**Fig 52** Cathedral window patchwork technique

a

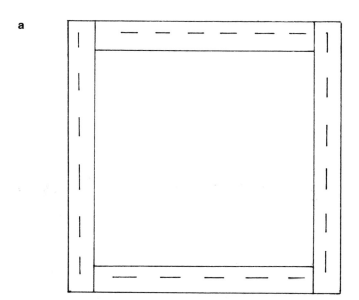

c

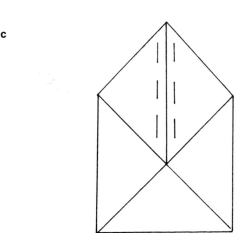

b

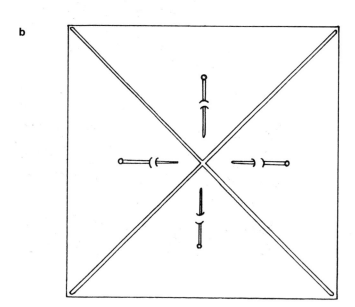

d

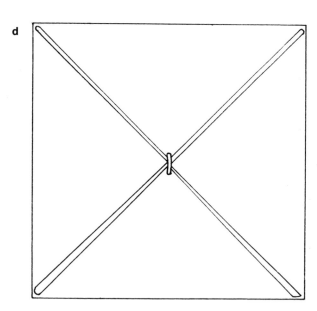

e

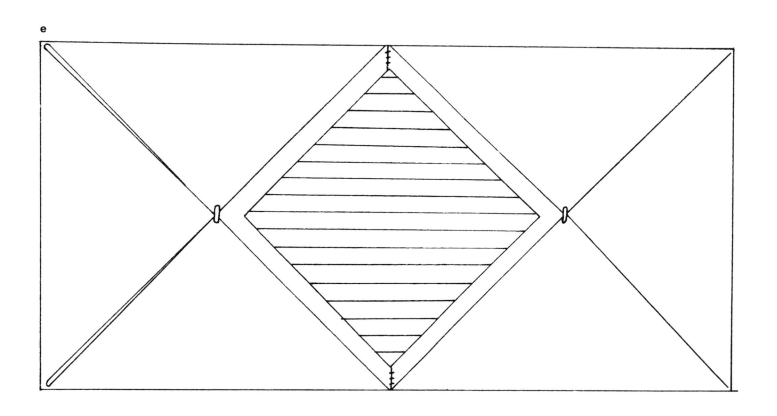

f

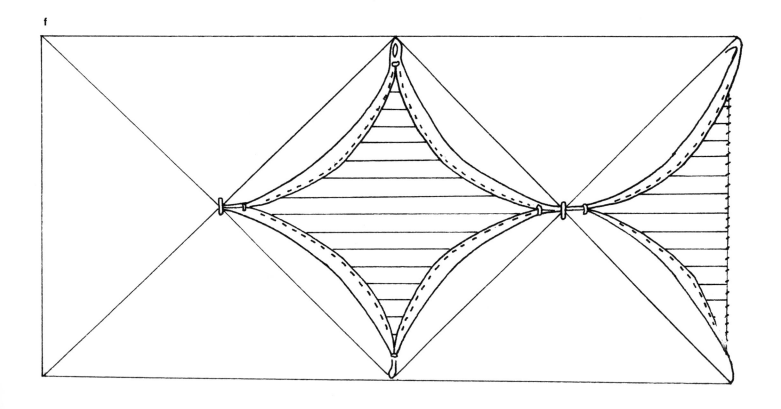

55

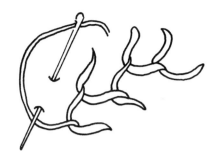

**Fig 53** Feather stitch

**Fig 54** Herringbone stitch

**Fig 55** Crazy patchwork

## Crazy patchwork

This method uses irregular shaped fabrics applied to a backing. Mark the required shapes on a pre-shrunk backing layer of calico or plain cotton. Cut out the fabric pieces on the straight grain and pin them, starting at one corner, overlapping the edges or turning under a narrow hem. Secure with small running stitches or by hemming. When all the patches have been secured, cover the edges of the shapes with decorative embroidery stitches – traditionally feather stitch (Fig 53) or herringbone stitch are used (Fig 54), but a machine zig-zag or satin stitch is also appropriate.

This technique lends itself to experiment because it is an effective method of combining materials of different weights and thicknesses such as silk/satin, and cotton/velvet. The patched surface can be further embellished with couched threads, beads, sequins and painted imagery, to form elaborate and decorative areas (Fig 55).

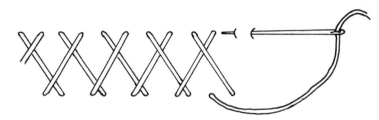

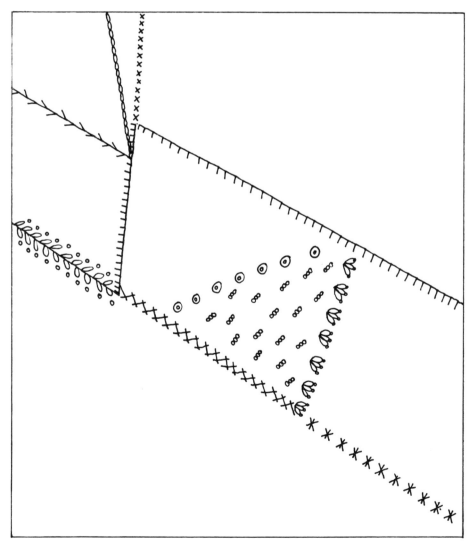

## Log cabin patchwork

This American technique depends upon the placing of light and dark strips arranged in sequence round a central square (Fig 56a). Cut strips of light and dark fabric approximately 3 cm wide, allowing 1 cm for turnings. The strips can be of any length, but the width must be consistently and accurately cut.

For each patch use a square piece of calico as a base. Pre-shrink the calico by washing, or by spraying with water and then ironing dry. Crease the square diagonally to find the centre and mark on the reverse side with a diagonal cross. Place a 6 cm square of fabric right side up so that each corner touches a diagonal line. Tack this down (Fig 56b). Mark pencilled numbers and lines on the reverse side of the foundation square as an aid to stitching.

Starting with side 1, place the first dark strip, cut to 6 cm long, right side down. Pin and machine stitch through the calico and strip 6 cm from the edge (Fig 56c). Cut the threads, turn the block over and press with an iron. Turn the block to side 2 and pin down the next dark strip. This should be the same length as the centre patch plus the width of the turned back first strip (Fig 56d). Sew down as for the first strip, and then press. Continue in the same way for sides 3 and 4, using pale fabrics instead of dark for the strips.

**Fig 56** Log cabin patchwork technique

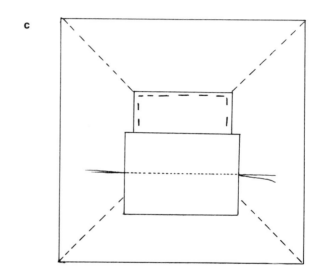

a

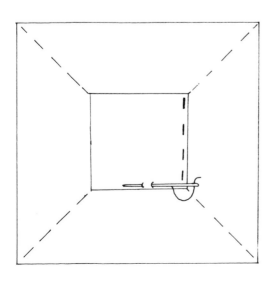

b

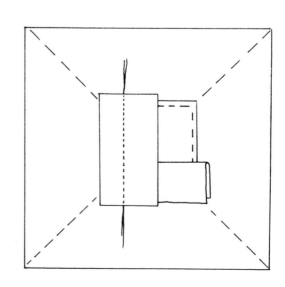

d

57

This completes the first round. Subsequent ones are done in the same way, always starting at side 1, but of course, the strips will be longer in each round (Fig 56e). The last four strips will be slightly wider than the others to allow a 1 cm turning which is necessary when the blocks are joined together (Fig 56f).

To join the blocks, place them on a clean, flat surface. Join by machine, into long strips, then join the strips together along the edge. Press the seams open.

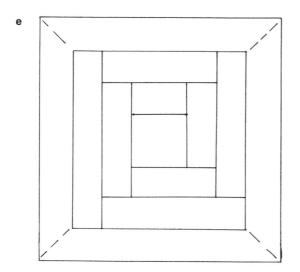

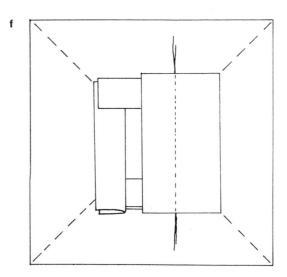

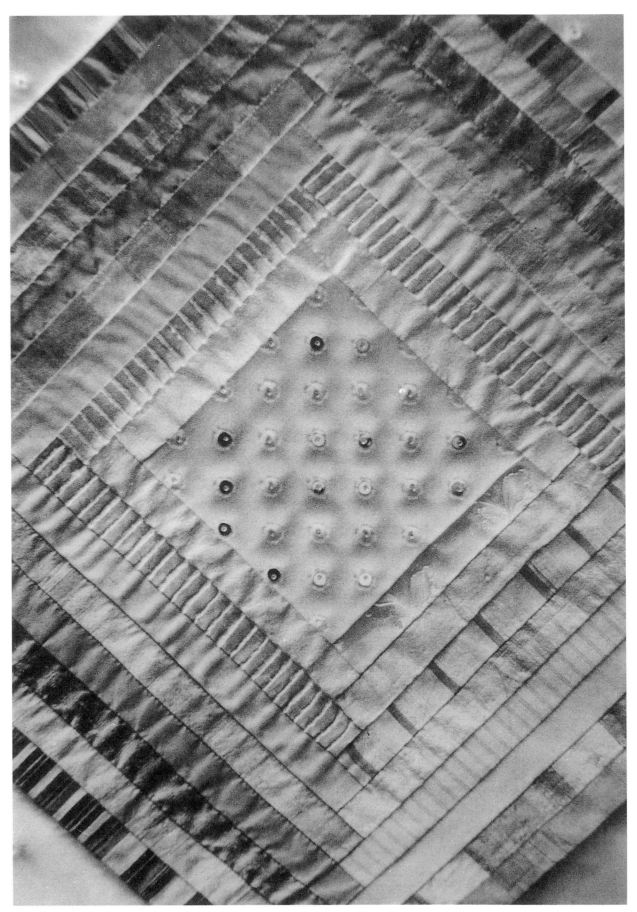

**Fig 57** Detail of log cabin patchwork
quilt (1985), Isabel Dibden-Wright

The log cabin block is of recurring interest to Isabel Dibden-Wright, and she often combines the tonal considerations of the design with carefully selected mixtures of fabrics: finely woven cottons, satin weaves, brocades and fine silks. The considered arrangements of the blocks are impeccably worked, demonstrating the artist's skilled needlework. A further embellishment in some work is her inclusion of hand-embroidered forms, often flowers, or surface stitchery, sometimes including sequins and beading (Fig 57). In other work, using her own variations on the log cabin technique, the artist uses strong bold contrasts of tone with restricted colour. In a commissioned quilt for Lord Rhodes, appliqué and quilted panels are executed in machine and hand stitchery, in black, white, red and green silk. These panels show representational images of his family life and activities, and are framed with log cabin piecing. The quilt border is in a white, green, red and black stripe pattern (Fig 58a).

Despite her love of stunning combinations of spectrum colours, the artist spends some time using neutral tones in her work, which act as periods of refreshment. The simple patterns of Amish quilts are an inspiration, and the artist has studied them in the United States. A striking quilt inspired partly by Amish patterns is *Patchwork 1980* (Fig 59). This is in

**Fig 58a** *Lord Rhodes Panel 2 : Japanese Gateway* (1983), Isabel Dibden-Wright

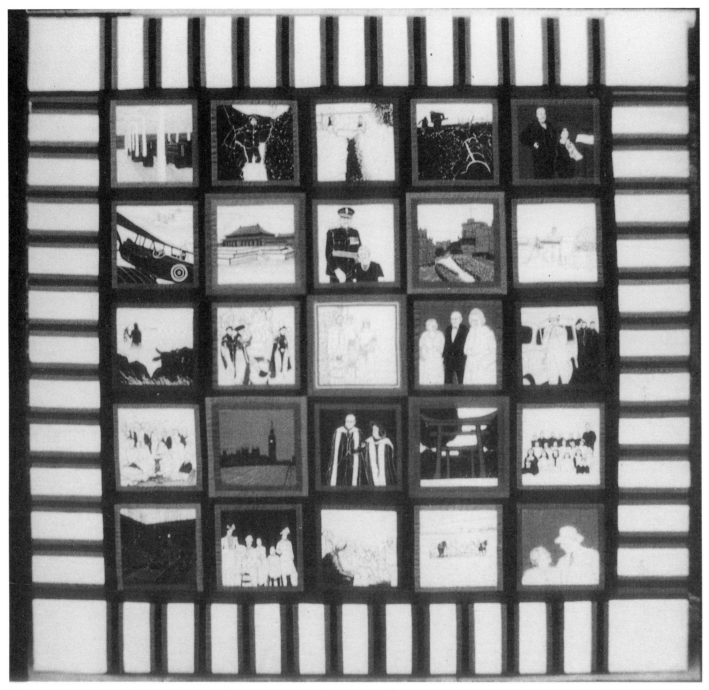

**Fig 58b** *Lord Rhodes Quilt* (1983), Isabel Dibden-Wright

fabric, using black, white and grey in different proportions, leading the eye to a single central red square. The use of limited colour in Isabel Dibden-Wright's work began at art college when the beautiful forms of flowers, particularly orchids, led her to produce a series of drawings using black and white so that she could realise effectively the particular tones and forms involved in their shape. When she works in strong colours, the artist sometimes abstracts those inspired by plants and flowers to use in log cabin designs, and she sometimes chooses to depict flowers representationally within the patchwork blocks (Fig 60).

Isabel Dibden-Wright combines her patchwork and quilting work as an artist with her position as Senior Lecturer in Embroidery at the Manchester Polytechnic Faculty of Art and Design, where she is a committed and much respected teacher. She considers that, in order to be effective, work needs to be carefully conceived and working methods require careful consideration in relation to the finished result. She stresses the importance of recognising that the source of work, which is in the mental and conceptual realm, and the working processes, which are in the physical realm, need to be combined carefully in order to produce physical results. The physical result (the work produced), whilst important, is only the remains of the creative process which precedes it, and therefore needs to be considered in conjunction with the preceding processes if it is to be excellent and satisfying.

Isabel Dibden-Wright lays emphasis on the organisation of the conceptual process and the physical making of pieces as the most important factors in their contribution to the finished result.

The artist's present work involves variations on Log Cabin blocks which use proportions reminiscent of Chinese lattices. She is presently interested in the changes of proportion she can achieve in their construction and in the use of strong colour contrast. Despite recent experimental excursions using traditional Japanese *ikat* fabrics, she anticipates that she will continue to develop her abiding fascination for using combinations of rich fabrics. Nuances of light reveal these qualities and invite exploration of the subtle artistry of Isabel Dibden-Wright's work.

**Fig 59** *Patchwork 1980*, Isabel Dibden-Wright

**Fig 60** A patchwork sample, Isabel
Dibden-Wright

# Communicating a wordless language

Whilst all art imparts a message, Dinah Prentice uses her work as a means of communicating the interest she has in language. She creates sewn constructions, with powerful scale, forms, and ideas, which are based upon philosophy, the power of language, and ideas relating to art and its place in contemporary life.

Educated in London at Haberdasher's Askes, and later at Wiggeston Girls Grammar School, Leicester, she remembers having an early interest

**Fig 61** *Brown Pineapple* (1978), Dinah Prentice

**Fig 62** *A4* (1979–80) 108″ × 156″, Dinah Prentice

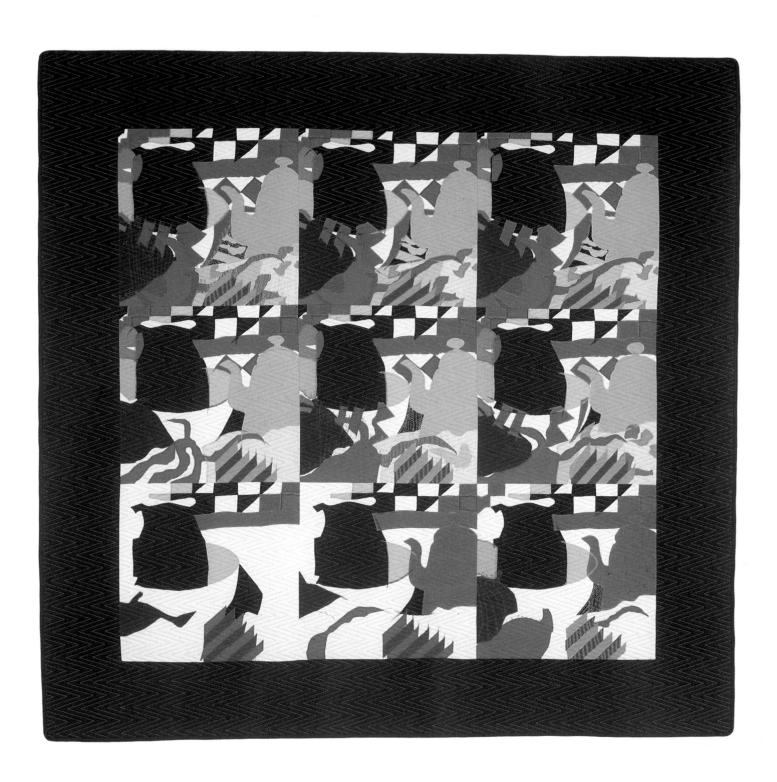

*Pink Teapot* (1987) 55″ × 55″, Pauline
Burbidge

*Indoor Kites* (1986) 18″ × 18″, Siripan
Kidd

*Self Reflective Text* (1985) 120″ × 144″,
Dinah Prentice

*Liverpool 2* (1987) 48″ × 60″, Eiluned
Edwards

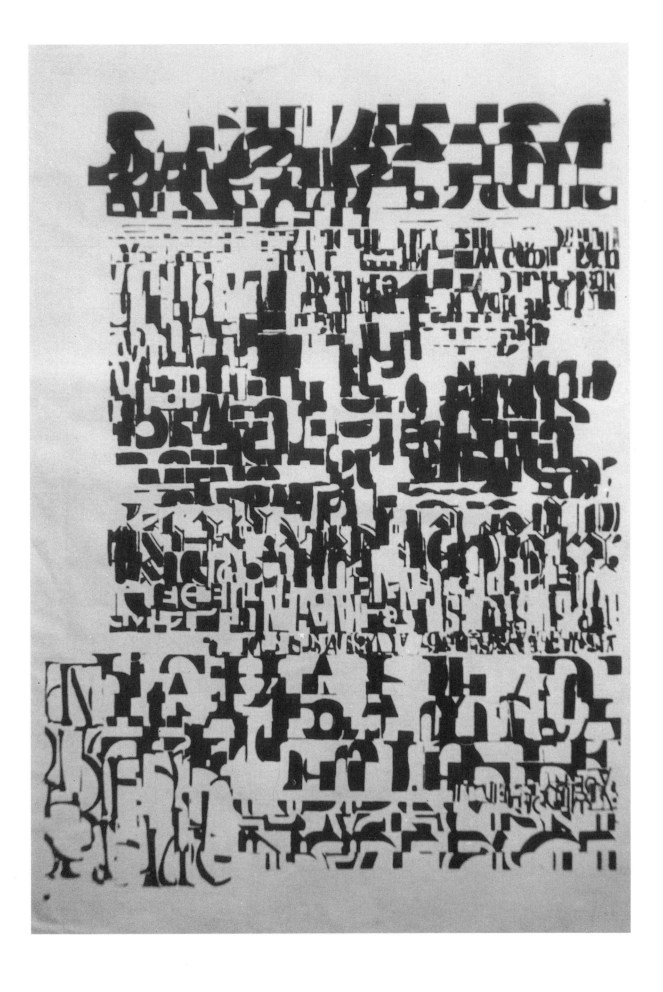

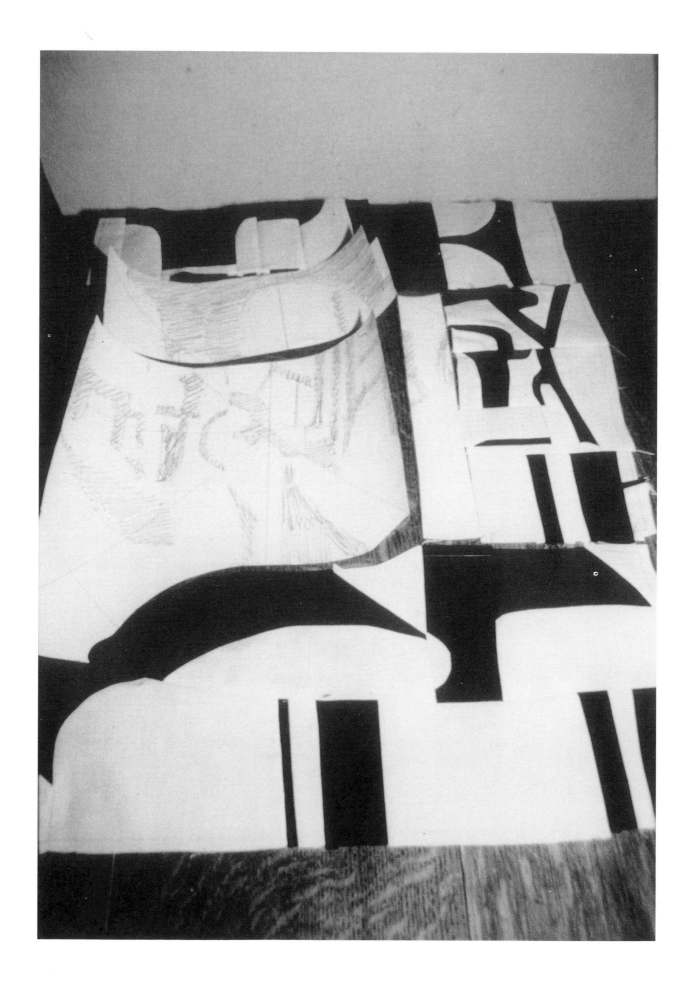

in the shape of letter forms, and the importance of a school prize, a book called *Life in the Old Stone Age* because these made her aware of different cultures. From schooldays she has always enjoyed graphs and maps because they represent the reinforcement of an idea with image. Her mother, a competent needlewoman, encouraged Dinah and her elder sister educationally. She encouraged Dinah's interests in research and experiment, and her later fine art education at Birmingham College of Art and the Academy Schools in London. Other early memories relating to her work are of being an evacuee during the war, and of visiting houses of widely travelled people in South London, whose ornaments contrasted with those of houses where there was nothing on display relating to foreign cultures.

After her art training, she led a busy life as a wife and mother of four children and was a joint founder of the Ikon Gallery in Birmingham, which involved organising exhibitions of contemporary work. She did some part-time teaching, and continued to produce a small range of prints and collages each year, most of which related to letter forms.

The first patchwork quilt she saw in 1975 led to her making some traditional quilts as a way of using up pieces of fabric and re-using the resources she had accumulated as part of the process of dressmaking for a growing family. She was encouraged to sell these quilts, which were made using traditional block patterns, and also to create some miniature samples, of which she made a set of five (Fig 61). The intricacies of this small-scale work, involving the use of two thousand densely arranged pieces of patchwork, convinced her that she was capable of attempting her first large, sewn construction, A4. This was a definitive work she had been considering for a year or more, involving the joining of forms less regular than those traditionally used in patchwork. It took two years to complete because she had to invent joining techniques as she went along. Subsequent works have been made much more quickly, as she became more proficient. A4 was produced from a collage piece which was made up of papers using letter forms (Fig 62).

## Patchwork with irregular shapes

Unlike crazy patchwork, which is applied to a background fabric, this method creates a fabric by piecing all the shapes together. A full-scale cartoon of the design is drawn, marking the main shapes on the paper using pencil. Dinah Prentice also makes a painting of the design, indicating tonal changes using shading in black and white or colour as appropriate.

The original cartoon is used as a pattern. Large radical cuts are made across the design and then these sections are sub-cut until she has a piece approximately 45 cm square. These smaller squares are then cut down to the last piecings and used as patterns. She cuts small pieces, one at a time, from the original paper design and, using these as patterns, cuts them out in fabric with a 6 mm seam allowance. As it is finished, each one is replaced in its correct place on the cartoon until it is completely replaced by the sewn pieces. She seams them together in areas by machine. Curved shapes need clipping at intervals to allow her to sew round complex curves. Dinah Prentice often sub-cuts shapes so that she can sew curved and rounded shapes together by machine.

The methods of patchwork construction used in A4 and related work have involved the artist developing a personal language of forms for her work. 'Language,' says Barthes, 'is power.' The users of language in any field have power over others. Dinah Prentice turned to the use of letter forms and written marks in her work both because she loves the way they are constructed, simply squares and triangles which encode all meanings, but also because she is shocked by the abuse of this simplicity. 'A mere

**Fig 63** *A4* technique showing enlarging grid. Fabric replaces paper. Dinah Prentice

scratch, tick or mark, and warrents are signed, treaties ratified, nations are thrown into debt, by the movement of marks from one column to another.' The forms Dinal Prentice uses are influenced by the Russian Constructivists Malcvitch and Tatlin, and, further west, Schwitters and Stella, but equally by literary ideas, including the structuralist philosophers such as Foucault and Barthes.

The relationship between drawing and designing and the construction of fabric lead to further works. After five years of working on lettering quilts, she began to shift the lettering forms in pictorial space, and to relate them to landscape, rather than translating the drawing straight into construction. She produced two drawings where she reversed her thinking, drawing the landscape objectively, using a series of written marks. These works have not been exhibited, but they had a radical influence on her thinking and work. She invests her design ideas with her current preoccupations.

*We three kings with rockets in our crowns*, a recent piece, is based upon American statistics showing that, of people who live near rocket sites, the men tend to approve of the missiles and the women do not. The artist was inspired by this information to produce a work showing rockets rising symbolically from the crowns of the figures. She made collages and drawings before finalising her design.

She is presently interested in hand colouring fabric, which is giving rise to painterliness. She dyes the fabric first, or paints the dye on to cloth with large brushes to give big marks, later cutting and joining the resultant areas of cloth. She retains her interest in the textiles produced by cultures which have a textile-based economy, particularly those of India, and in the marks and forms which relate to them. These interests may become apparent in her current work.

The soft, durable forms of quilts have appeal for the artist and wadding, backing, tying and binding techniques are considered essential elements in finished works. Indeed one of the difficulties of transporting very large stretched canvases was solved by making sewn constructions. Dinah Prentice enjoys working on a large scale, and she is also concerned with the amount of energy invested in the making of sewn construction because it allows time for the development of her ideas (Fig 64).

As well as this commitment to ideas and concepts, Dinah Prentice is examining the tradition of women creating domestic wealth. Definitions of Fine Art are often constructed in such a way that many of the works produced by women are excluded, because of their content, their level of expression, or, very often, because of the medium employed. Thus, a traditional bed quilt is not an object generally accepted as falling within the context of Fine Art.

Fabric is a material to which women have always related because of the activities of making, sewing, washing and so on, either traditionally or by choice. Dinah Prentice has ideas about women's roles in relation to art and design which cannot be simply and easily labelled as feminist, and more than her work can be dismissed as a woman's medium. By examining the different forms of quilts, the relationship between textile and design and creating an effective art language can be made clearer. Since textile design is one of the few areas of female artistic prominence, the medium of quilts is an ideal vehicle to promote and explore these ideas. Dinah Prentice goes further when she states that she feels deepest despair when faced with the monotonous self-satisfaction and retrogressive content of many of the quilts she has seen produced and exhibited. Put simply, the meaning or content of any work is the springboard for that work and the material provides only the means to those ends. Dinah Prentice finds sewn constructions the most malleable means to achieve her ends. She quotes

**Fig 64** Sewn construction exhibition at Milton Keynes 1984. Dinah Prentice

Naum Gabo, 'We construct our work as the universe constructs its own'. She wants her art to be not merely a representation, but a unique reconstruction of our life concerns.

# Personal development

Mary Fogg states that, as well as colour and traditional patterns of natural forms, she would like to see quiltmakers tackle personal themes and new formulas. She believes that the quilt movement cannot stand still: it must include people taking risks and pushing out the boundaries of the craft. It was because of this that she helped to form Quilt Art, to encourage artists to explore new boundaries in quiltmaking. Her own work concerns structural considerations of cloth through the use of strip patchwork. Colour and tone are subtly integrated into her finished works, which are now hanging wall-pieces (Fig 65).

An Old Testament description of the Israelites' tent made a great impression on her when she was a small child. The account was of the Israelites' journey from Egypt to the Promised Land, and the tent was their Tabernacle, described as being lined with coloured and richly-embroidered cloth. The image presented is still vivid to her now, and it fired her imagination then. Mary Fogg wanted to train as a textile designer, but this was not possible in wartime England. She therefore trained in fine art at the Slade in London, leaving before her course ended to join the Women's Army Service. After a few years working in educational films she married, had a family, and spent the next few years travelling in Canada.

During her sojourn in Canada she came across North American quilts and wanted to learn how to make them. With little basic knowledge of method, she bought some square cards and cottons during a holiday journey and made a very unsatisfactory cushion cover. A break in her interest followed, during which time she experimented with embroidery and fabric collage as a member of the Beckenham Textile Studio. Her first quilt was made for her son's room when he redecorated and needed a durable bedcover. She made this using a mixture of scrap materials in brown and gold, corduroy, crepe, wool, cotton velvet and woven cotton mixtures, to give a ploughed-field effect. The method she used was strip patchwork, machined in one operation through wadding and backing to make a quick, economical and tough quilt of interesting appearance. The sewing took longer than expected, but she had stumbled on a method of using fabric in the way she wanted, because the three-dimensional pattern which resulted seemed to blend the different textured cloths, giving an informal richness not possible when using only one kind of fabric.

She enjoys using the great range of cloths available today, and usually uses old fabrics from charity shops. Old clothes offer her a wider range of pattern and colour than the limited annual fashion colour ranges which are available in new textiles. Her use of colour is personal, and is influenced by

**Fig 65** *Odeon* (1984), Mary Fogg

**Fig 66** *Red Centre of Australia with Cow* (1985), Mary Fogg

works by Monet and other Impressionists, and the colouring, textures, and pattern changes in old Persian carpets.

She works in different scales, miniature and bedsize, exploiting edges, making them frayed to blend colour and hard-edged to emphasise line in other areas. Small sample collages of silk strips applied with spray mount adhesive are used to develop larger panel ideas. The possibilities offered by the strip unit are something she enjoys exploring and, by developing her interest in this through the use of different fabrics, her work has a continuity on which to build.

She also draws inspiration from the natural world, extracting ideas of colour, textural and light effects and recreating them in terms of strip patchwork. Her recent work has been a series called *The Red Centre* (Fig 66), inspired by the Australian landscape around Alice Springs on a ten-day holiday in a campervan. She has aimed to express, in pieces of cloth, the landscape, colour and space of the desert. This involved a number of technical experiments to make wall quilts which suggest an untidy untamed quality, but would be durable and could be handled without damage. She hopes to exploit these in later work.

Mary Fogg sees quiltmaking as a traditional craft, but she considers it important to attempt to increase public awareness that the form is also carrying contemporary ideas. She sees this as involving a degree of desertion of beds for walls, along with a professional level of commitment – a slow, but important, process.

# Handsewn patchwork: the technique which frees expression

Joe Boyle trained at Glasgow College of Art, where he obtained the Diploma in Art. After his initial first-year general course at the college, he felt he needed more time to decide on his main course of study, and looked for an area in which he could work with a broad range of materials, eventually choosing murals and stained glass, with embroidery and weaving as subsidiary subjects. During the course, working under Hannah Frew Patterson, Chrissy White and Kath White, he turned increasingly to embroidery and weaving, finding in them the potential to develop graphic and linear design ideas which interested him.

He discovered patchwork through learning the technique of English joining at college. This method irritated him, and he considered it primitive because it was time-consuming and led to puckering of the fabric. He produced three major pieces based on hexagons for a project at college. The inspiration for these pieces was a picture of German bombers camouflaged in the First World War with grey, orange, and green nets and coloured paint. Joe Boyle used these colours in the three-dimensional pieces he created: adapting the Suffolk puff patchwork technique, he stretched thick nylon lining material over card templates and attached the fabric with Sellotape, before stitching the patches together by hand. The second piece was also a three-dimensional nylon construction in red, blue and black, designed to be suspended.

He sees drawing as important, and personally appreciates the detailed work of Albert Durer and Picasso. Without the ability to draw, the artist is unable to find the images he wishes to use. His training in drawing allows him to recognise the images he needs, and it gives him experience in seeking out the right image to express the idea. When Joe Boyle is searching for an image to express the idea. When Joe Boyle is searching for an image, drawing allows him to plan, to get it wrong, to see whether the figure and ground will work. It is important for him to get his ideas right so that a piece will work for him, because he has limited time. Drawing is a method used by the artist as a stage in evolving a piece, but it is a planning and contributing factor. Of itself, in relation to the finished pieces, drawing is temporal.

Joe Boyle also has no qualms about the way he designs in terms of observation skills. He searches for images to fit his current ideas, and he lifts images from the television screen by freezing video frames, or from photographs. These are traced on to acetate, or projected, to enlarge them, and drawn straight on to card. Sometimes he changes images during the drawing process, or cuts two images on the video and combines them.

**Fig 67** *You Can't Hide an Army* (1978)
48″ × 48″, Joe Boyle

**Fig 68** *Chrissy* (1979) 48″ × 64″, Joe Boyle

The idea of using patchwork was born out of a desire to improve upon technique, and this interest in technique also relates to his successful business in stained glass. During the last few years, he has produced many one-off pieces in stained glass, and built up commercial and production export lines which are based upon Tiffany, Art Nouveau and designs of the Scottish architect Mackintosh. Whilst his quilts offer him a kind of solace from this work, which is based upon the need to earn a living, he sees analogies between the two activities. In both glass and patchwork the approach is graphic, and the template system is the same. The glass-cutting tool for glass becomes the scissors for patchwork; the diamond router joins glass, whilst the sewing machine or handstitching join fabric. The cotton-tape solder acts as a thread for glass, whilst cotton thread holds together fabric.

Pieces of patchwork are a method the artist uses to create his own personal space, and, whilst he is aware of their commercial possibilities and exhibits to sell, he produces pieces not in order to sell them, but for himself. His subject matter is wholly influenced by the media and the way the world is presented to us in newspapers and on television. Joe Boyle's main artistic influence is the work of Allan Jones, the British pop artist of the 1960s, but he is influenced by British and American pop art generally, because it was an art movement with impact. Pop artists presented strong pieces of work which demanded a reaction and made people stop and think.

**'The technique'**

The foundation of Joe Boyle's patchwork is the simple technique he has devised to piece together his work. From the thin card on which he has drawn or traced the design image, he cuts pieces out, and uses these directly as a template. These templates are stronger than paper, but still light and pliable. He wraps fabric around the template, showing no concern for straight edges, warp or weft, and attaches the fabric to the card with small pieces of Sellotape, trimming the seam allowance as he works. The pieces are oversewn by hand using a very fine needle and black cotton thread. He favours black thread because the very nature of the piecing process creates a line, so why attempt to hide it?

The technique is a joy because it is such a direct progression from design or drawing, but, more than this, it gives the patchworker the freedom to deal with expressive and complicated shapes and curves with ease. The pieces are also portable, and so work can be undertaken anywhere.

Some pieces are left unlined, but the larger pieces have borders which relate in colour and proportion to the images used. The size suggests itself in relation to the idea that the artist wishes to present. Some of the patchworks are made up as lined quilts, but the artist does not use wadding or quilting in their construction.

Joe Boyle recognises the creative strength of hand-stitching. He appreciates the beauty of much traditional British and American quilting and patchwork which was technologically advanced for its time. He considers that a great deal of modern British patchwork has followed standard formulas. This may be because of people following geometric patterns and being limited by geometry, or, as he sees it, a relationship between the work produced and money factors. People have followed the line of least resistance when designing and making quilts, producing garish and ill-conceived work, instead of interpreting intensely felt personal feelings and images into the medium. Joe Boyle sees his technique as a freeing device for people working in patchwork.

A recurring theme in the artist's patchwork pieces continues to relate to

**Fig 69** Image transfer technique, Joe Boyle

camouflage, and to how soldiers and armies, in so-called 'camouflage' uniforms, are in fact easy to see, and therefore become easy targets for gunmen. This poses questions about the role of armies, whether they are there as a show of force, or merely as victims of aggression. A piece which developed from these thoughts is *You can't hide an army*. It is in cotton fabrics of grey, tan and green, and depicts a soldier in Belfast against a patterned background (Fig 67). Joe Boyle quotes from W. B. Yates' poem about war and the Easter Rising, *A terrible beauty is born*.

Much of Joe Boyle's work includes figures, sometimes of his family, e.g. *Chrissy* (Fig 68), which depicts his wife against a patterned background. Working in a traditional medium has given Joe Boyle the opportunity to realise the importance of human tradition. He cites Leakie the archaeologist and his discoveries of early man, not as an aggressive being who feared fellow human beings, but as a happy and free person. The artist sees an importance in the traditional ways people live, particularly in those traditions relating to day-to-day living. This has given rise to work on the theme of new towns, which he deprecates, and his personal comment on the way in which an environment (sometimes even artwork, such as painted gable-end designs) is imposed upon people without their participation or approval. This theme is dealt with in a series of small patchworks which are pieced in complicated shapes.

In almost all his work the artist uses plain cotton fabrics, buying every year, or sometimes twice a year, from local shops and markets, to get a wide, rather than a fashionable, palette of colours. He stores the fabric in polythene bags, and selects the piece he requires when he begins a new piece of work. The flesh tones in his figures are usually presented in flesh-toned cotton, with the pattern of the patchwork piecing working across the image.

Recently, the artist has experimented with transferring actual images onto cloth by using shellac varnish to coat colour pictures from magazines. Whilst this is still wet, cloth is pressed against the varnish with hand pressure and the image transfers faintly to the cloth. This technique has led to a small piece (Fig 69) in which a figure in the foreground representing Western values is seen against the transfer-printed background piecing taken from photographs of Ethiopian refugees and rotting carcasses in the African desert. This method of transferring imagery was also used during the 1960s by the American pop artist Robert Rauschenberg.

Joe Boyle thinks that much of the art which is produced has little impact. About his own work he says, 'my work won't change things, but there is self-satisfaction in creating my own space'.

# The studio: an inspirational working environment

The Swiss quilt artist Radka Donnell has been reported as saying that the reason quilts are important to her is because they provide a place where she has her own space. She cites how many women have to follow their husbands or fathers around, and are thus limited in their choice of the kind of house or place they want to live in. They can find, in the arrangement of patchwork, and in the making of quilts, a place where they can make their own decisions about space. She says that in learning to make decisions about placement of pieces and colours, she gained a lot of confidence in her decision-making ability in other areas of her life. She also considers that it is important for quilts to be used as quilts. Many quilts can be used only as wall-hangings. It is important, she says, to be able to wrap yourself in her quilts. The touch element is also very important to her, and she sees quilting as a very comforting kind of thing for that reason.

It was with these comments on the importance of personal space in mind that I asked all the artists how and where they liked to work. Since the studio situation was seen by many to be important in relation to their work, this section is presented with the artist's own words alongside pictures of them in their working areas.

**A space to work: Deirdre Amsden**

'Over the years I have graduated from working on the dining table, to a corner of the sitting room to a workroom with little daylight, to the top room of a converted Victorian temperance chapel and now to my present studio in the East End of London. It is one of many studios being developed in an old factory complex. The Docklands Light Railway runs under my windows on one side and on the other they open onto a small patio and roof garden beyond.

It is an ideal workshop, light, airy and quiet with a pleasant atmosphere. I am not a tidy worker so I like the plain walls and wooden beams and the wood floor provides me with another work surface which I use every bit as much as the large table I have constructed from two flush doors resting on trestles. The arrangement of furniture and equipment is spaced out as I like the luxury of walking between various areas as I work. I only tidy up when I have finished a piece of work or have a mini tidy between the various stages of making a quilt.

I have always adapted to the space available to me, but this has been easy as each has been an improvement on the last. However I like to think, should circumstances change, that I would be equally adaptable to less favourable surroundings again. Being able to work *somewhere* is my first concern, that I work somewhere so agreeable at the moment is a bonus.'

**Pauline Burbidge**

'I now work in a large studio space which I have used since June '86. Previously to this I always worked in a very confined space, a room in my house. The move to larger premises seemed essential when I began to use the industrial quilting method, this process meant that I could produce many more works each year.

Having a larger space has meant that I can critically view the work while in progress, stand back from it and observe, then decide on the next move. I feel that this allows me to work more spontaneously with fabric, whereas before, in a confined space, I worked from small-scale designs and relied on these to give me an indication of the appearance of the finished work. Before having the studio, it seemed that I didn't really get to look at my work properly until it was exhibited!'

**Christine Mitchell**

'In the early stages of making a wall-hanging I work in my studio where I do all my "dirty work", dyeing fabrics, also I like to make paper collages and paintings from my source material this I like to do away from others. I like to "paint along" to a vigorous piece of music on the radio. The stitching I do in my home, preferably with the company of my family or friends.'

**Esther Barratt**

'I very much need to work with other people. I rent a workspace at the Cirencester Workshops, where other craftsmen also have workspaces. I find it very stimulating when everyone is working hard on our different crafts. Sometimes other people can be a distraction, but the disadvantages are nothing compared with the advantages. It's good to sound out new ideas with them and a good discipline to advise them on their work when they ask for it. People are important and it's good to have them around.'

**Isabel Dibden-Wright**

'I need to work in a quiet, ordered environment. Good light is essential, and a certain amount of space. The most important space and calm needs to exist in the mental world, more so than in the physical work, so I speak about subtle qualities. The work can only be undertaken on an irregular basis as the pattern of life exists for me now. The work needs to be done in a measured way, with full attention being given, and from a point of stillness within. Work undertaken without stillness and attention is always second-rate. I consider the way people work to be most revealing about the nature of the work they produce.'

**Eiluned Edwards**

'I'm a territorial creature, I'd like a studio. I'm adjusting to thinking of myself as an artist, so a studio fits that idea. The size of the work I'm producing needs a large working area – in my present flat I've taken over because of this, but I don't want to encroach on other people's space, so an independent working area is a necessity. I enjoy working on my own, it enables me to reflect upon my work undisturbed, but other people are an important stimulus.

Contact with other interested groups who are piecemaking will always be important.'

**Liz Bruce**

'I like my work ideas to flow in a fluid situation, not necessarily in the studio.'

**Mary Fogg**

'My workroom is the attic room at the top of our house, where I work surrounded by my "paint boxes", clear plastic bags, boxes, and cupboards full of different pieces of cloth, old and new, which are filed according to type of material and colour. It is difficult to prevent these stocks encroaching on my working space. I would like space for a really big table and, even more walls, high enough to design big works against them and see them from a distance. But I love my room at tree-top level.'

**Dinah Prentice**

'I work in a studio in my own home, it is in a central area of the house with kitchen and living room easily accessible. Having spent years training myself to work in short bursts, between demands of family, I find it a hard habit to shake off, and I still like to manage a household in between working.'

### Siripan Kidd

'I need to treat my work seriously, so I have to have a room of my own with good light and space. I put in six to seven hours a day, and, if I happen to be interrupted in the day, I try to make up the time in the evening. Sometimes I have to sit up until one or two o'clock to finish certain pieces. It is hard work physically and mentally. You can feel isolated working on your own, but when people make good comments on your work it is a great opportunity to share your excitement.'

### Joe Boyle

'I create space for myself by making the pieces, meditating if you like, although I'm not strictly into mystic forces. I can work anywhere, because of the freedom the technique gives, and because of the portability of the pieces, in the studio, at home, watching television or on top of a bus.'

**Andrea Fothergill**

'The studio is a spacious and inspirational room which is in constant use. It houses television, stereo and comfortable chairs along with working equipment. Current work is always in view, so that fresh evaluations can be made. There are wide ranges of fabrics, threads and graphic materials available which have been collected over many years. These materials are carefully stored, and colour coded, to reduce time when making selections. Freely available graphic materials, fabrics and threads are provocative and inspirational to me. I have adequate table space, but have to be well organised to maintain a working situation. Correct and adequate lighting is very important. The work area is situated near a bay window and the natural light is supplemented by three different types of fixture, "anglepoise," spotlight and striplight. I like to be warm and I enjoy both working and relaxing in my studio, it offers every possible need and comfort.'

# Further reading

BETTERTON, Sheila — *Quilts and Coverlets from the American Museum in Britain*, The American Museum in Britain, Bath, 1978

BEYER, Jinny — *Patchwork Patterns*, Bell & Hyman, 1982

BURBIDGE, Pauline — *Making Patchwork for Pleasure and Profit*, John Gifford, 1981

COLBY, Averil — *Patchwork/Quilting*, Batsford Craft Paperback Series, B. T. Batsford, 1983

FINLEY, Ruth — *Old Patchwork Quilts and the Women who Made Them*, Newton Centre, Massachusetts, Charles T. Branford Co, 1971

HOLSTEIN, Jonathan — *The Pieced Quilt and American Design Tradition*, New York Graphic Society, 1973

LUBELL, Cecil — *Textile Collections of the World, Volume 2, United Kingdom – Ireland*, Studio Vista, London, 1976

MCMORRIS, Penny — *Quilting: an Introduction to American Patchwork Design*, BBC, 1984

OSLER, Dorothy — *Machine Patchwork Technique and Design*, B. T. Batsford, 1980

OSLER, Dorothy — *Traditional British Quilts*, B. T. Batsford, 1987

ROBINSON, Charlotte — *The Artist and the Quilt*, Quarto Marketing Ltd, 1983

RUSH, Beverley (with LASSIE Witman) — *The Complete Book of Seminole Patchwork*, Madrona Publishers Inc, 1982

SHORT, Eirian — *Quilting Technique, Design and Application*, B. T. Batsford, 1979

WALKER, Michele — *Quiltmaking in Patchwork and Appliqué*, Ebury Press, 1985

# Suppliers, guilds, etc

**Devon**
Strawberry Fayre, Chagford, Newton Abbot, Devon TQ13 8EN
Tel: 06473 3250

*English, European and American cotton fabrics, wadding and quilt making supplies. Mail order only; SAE for catalogue.*

**Dorset**
The Patchwork Shoppe, The Old Mill, 13 Mill Lane, Wimborne, Dorset
Tel: 0202 881240

*Fabrics, templates, hoops, wadding, English and American books. Mail order service available for fabrics; SAE for samples.*

**London**
John Lewis, Oxford Street, London W1 (also provincial branches)
Tel: 01-629 7711

*Large selection of fabrics including habotai silk; also wadding, thread, binding, kits, haberdashery. Mail order service available for fabrics.*

McCulloch & Wallis Ltd, 25–26 Derring Street, London W1R 0BE
Tel: 01-129 0311

*Wadding, fabric, thread, needles, vilene 'Patchwork Secret'. Mail order service available.*

**Scotland**
Midlothian Textile Workshop and Gallery, Gladstone's Lane, Lawnmarket, Edinburgh
Tel: 031-225 4570

*Templates, wadding, threads, books etc.*

**Ireland**
Design workshop, 162 Portaferry Road, Newtownards, Co. Down
Tel: 024 774 422

*Patchwork kits, quilting designs, templates etc. SAE for stock list.*

Quilt Art Accessory, The Hill House, Tippen Road, Naas, Co. Kildare, Ireland
Tel: 045 76121

## Fabrics

**London**
S. Borovick, 16 Berwick Street, London W1
Tel: 01-437 2180

*Large range of fabrics, theatrical fabrics.*

Pongées Ltd, 184–186 Old Street, London EC1
Tel: 01-253 0428

*Importers of pure silk in natural state for printing and dyeing.*

George Weil & Sons Ltd, 63–65 Riding House Street, London W1P 7PP
Tel: 01-580 3763

*Pure silk and cotton fabrics suitable for dyeing and printing, also 'Super Tinfix' paints for silk and wool. SAE for price list and samples.*

**Yorkshire**
Whaleys (Bradford) Ltd, Harris Court Mills, Great Horton, Bradford, West Yorkshire BD7 4EQ
Tel: 0274 576718

*A wide range of assorted fabrics for printing and dyeing. Mail order only, SAE for price list.*

**Scotland**
The Cloth Shop, 24 Craighill Road, Edinburgh
Tel: 031-552 8818

*Fabrics and haberdashery.*


## Books and magazines

Craft Publications, 104 Salford Road, Aspley Guise, Milton Keynes, Buckinghamshire, MK17 8H2
Tel: 0908 582743

*American quilt and patchwork magazines* **Quilt**, **Quilters' Newsletter**, **Fibre Arts**, *etc. Also books and patterns. SAE for subscription details.*

Bayswater Books, 112a Westbourne Grove, London W2 5RU
Tel: 01-229 1432

*Textile craft books and periodicals.*


## Specialist quilt cleaning

The White Fleece, 16–17 Glendower Place, London SW7
Tel: 01-584 1246

*Specialist dry cleaners. SAE for details.*


## Auction houses and galleries
## Sales of antique patchwork and quilts

**London**
Christie's (South Kensington), 85 Old Brompton Road, London SW7
Tel: 01-581 7611

*Regular auctions of textiles, quilts and needlework.*

**Worcestershire**
Andrew Grant Fine Art, Auctioneers, 59 Foregate Street, Worcester
Tel: 0905 52310

*Sales of antique patchwork.*

**Scotland**
Christie's Scotland, 164 Bath Street, Glasgow
Tel: 041-332 8134

*Regular auctions of textiles, quilts and needlework.*

Philips, 65 George Street, Edinburgh
Tel: 031-225 2266

*Specialist sale twice yearly.*


## London specialist shops selling antique and modern quilts

Appalachian Designs, 157 St Johns Hill, London SW11
Tel: 01-228 3913

Gallery of Antique Costume and Textiles, 2 Church Street, London NW8
Tel: 01-723 9981

Liberty Regent Street, London W1
Tel: 01-734 9981

*A selection of modern patchwork and quilts.*


## Museum collections

Quilts are often kept in reserve collections for research and study purposes. It is always advisable to arrange an appointment before a visit.

### Avon
The American Museum in Britain, Claverton Manor, Bath, Avon BA2 7BD
Tel: 0225 60503 (Education Dept 63538)

*Large collection of American quilts.*

### Cumbria
Levens Hall, Kendal, Cumbria LA8 0PB
Tel: 0448 60321

*The earliest English patchwork quilt (circa 1708) and other fine needlework.*

### Durham
North of England Open Air Museum, Beamish, Stanley, Co. Durham
Tel: 0207 31811

*One of the finest collections of quilts in Britain, some on view, others by arrangement with the Keeper of Social History.*

The Bowes Museum, Barnard Castle, Co. Durham
Tel: 0833 37139

*Another fine collection of quilts, viewing by arrangement with the Curator.*

### Lancashire
Gawthorpe Hall, Padiham, Nr Burnley, Lancashire BB12 8UA
Tel: 0282 78511

*The Rachel Kay-Shuttleworth collection of embroidery, lace and costume including 60 quilts dating from the eighteenth century to the present day. Available for personal study by arrangement with the Curator.*

### London
Victoria and Albert Museum, Cromwell Road, South Kensington, London SW7 2RL
Tel: 01-589 6371

*Small collection of quilts on view. Quilts in store available for personal study by arrangement with the Keeper, Department of Textiles.*

### Norfolk
Strangers Hall, Charing Cross, Norwich, Norfolk NR2 4AL
Tel: 0603 611277, extension 275

*Approximately fifty quilts in collection. View by arrangement with the curator.*

**Sussex**
Worthing Museum and Art Gallery, Chapel Road, Worthing, West Sussex
Tel: 0903 39999, ext 121

*About 40 quilts to view by arrangement with Assistant Curator of Costume.*

**Wales**
South Glamorgan
Welsh Folk Museum, St Fagans, Cardiff CF5 6XB
Tel: 0222 569441

*Some items may be viewed on request to Head of Department, domestic and corporate life.*

**Scotland**
Royal Scottish Museum, Chambers Street, Edinburgh EH1 1JF
Tel: 031-225 7534

**Northern Ireland**
Ulster Folk and Transport Museum, Cultra Manor Holywood, County Down
BT18 0EU
Tel: 023 17 5411

*Large collection of quilts and coverlets. Reserve collection can be viewed by arrangement with the Keeper, Department of Textiles.*


## Quilting guilds and groups

**The Quilters' Guild**
An organisation for quiltmakers which aims to promote through education and demonstration a greater understanding, appreciation and knowledge of the art, techniques and heritage of patchwork, appliqué and quilting.

For membership details contact:
The Secretary
Margaret Petit
56 Wilcolt Road
Pewsey
Wiltshire SN9 5EL

**Quilt Art**
For further details contact:
Christine Mitchell
9 South Close
Hatch End
Pinner
Middx
Tel: 01-868 3910

**Scottish Quilters' Guild**

**Irish Quilters' Guild**

**Irish Patchwork Society**

# 15

# Index